SENIOR
DOG

THE
SENIOR
DOG

Heike Schmidt-Röger
Susanne Blank

LONDON, NEW YORK,
MELBOURNE, MUNICH, AND DELHI

For Dorling Kindersley, Munich:
Publishing Manager Monika Schlitzer
Managing Editor Regina Franke
Production Manager Dorothee Whittaker
DTP Designer Verena Salm
Jacket Design Verena Salm

For DK Publishing
Senior Editor Jill Hamilton

Adapted from the German by:
International Book Productions Inc.,
Toronto, Canada
Translated by Barbara Hopkinson

First American Edition, 2007

Published in the United States by
DK Publishing, 375 Hudson Street
New York, NY 10014

07 08 09 10 11 10 9 8 7 6 5 4 3 2 1

SD232—July 2007

A Cataloging-in-Publication record for this book is available from
the Library of Congress.
ISBN: 978-0-7566-2206-0

DK books are available at special discounts for bulk purchases for sales promotions, premiums,
fund-raising, or educational use. For details, contact: DK Publishing Special Markets,
375 Hudson Street, New York, NY 10014 or SpecialSales@dk.com

Color reproduction by medienservice farbsatz,
Neuried, Germany
Printed and bound in Singapore by Tien Wah

Discover more at
www.dk.com

CONTENTS

INTRODUCTION

Dogs are considered to be man's best friend and truest companion. From the moment a dog joins our family, it places its well-being in our hands. We accompany our dog throughout every phase of its life and must be ready and willing to deal with the various needs of our special friend as it ages. Particularly when a dog reaches old age, loving care is a special challenge.

When you ask dog owners which years with their companions were the best, the answer is often the last phase of their dog's life, a time when a close relationship has developed between human and dog and communicating with one another requires few words.

For many years we have shared our lives with dogs—with those that grew old at our sides and those who won our hearts when they were already going gray. We felt exactly the same way about them all. Senior dogs are simply wonderful. Showing consideration for their diminished powers and caring for them when they become ill is not a duty but a labor of love that we perform happily. Looking into the eyes of our dogs and enjoying our shared walks together is the best repayment for us.

Our aim in this book is to give answers to commonly asked questions about keeping a dog healthy, provide tips, and help owners of senior dogs better understand their companions and enjoy their precious time together.

Susanne Blank

Heike Schmidt-Röger

AGE IS RELATIVE

IN THE PAST, DOGS often worked at demanding and tiring jobs. Certainly many of them were "happier" then since they had jobs to perform that suited their natures and kept them totally occupied. However, when they could no longer perform their duties, they were not always allowed to live to a ripe old age in their habitual surroundings as a matter of course.

Things are quite different today. The life expectancy of dogs has increased and most dogs are family dogs, living to a ripe old age at the side of their owners, lavished with care and attention. However, often their abilities and desire to perform is underestimated and they are relegated much too early to the scrap heap.

Senior dogs definitely can still contribute to their two and four-legged packs and they very much want to be included. They want to be physically challenged as much as possible. However, it is not always easy for an owner to gauge what activities a senior canine housemate is still capable of doing, or when too much is expected of it, since the aging process differs in every individual.

WHAT DOES AGING MEAN?

A DOG TALE

Joschi, my Retriever-mix, started to get gray hairs on his muzzle very early on in life, when he was just four. He's now ten and still in top form. He loves to be included in everything I do and I sometimes even have to put on the brakes so that he doesn't overdo it. But a life on the sofa and no action—this would be unthinkable for Joschi!

Even when a dog can no longer physically perform in the same way as in its younger years, an old dog is not necessarily an ill dog, and getting old is not an illness.

Aging is a physiological change to the body that occurs later in life. Biochemical processes play a great role in aging.

In the course of time, the way cells, tissues, internal organs and other parts of a dog's body function alters for the worse. Its ability to cope with change of any kind diminishes. There are many signs of this deterioration. For example, its immune system becomes less efficient, leading to a greater number of infections and perhaps cancerous tumors. Its ability to learn new things declines, as does its level of physical fitness and agility. It might tire more easily and so is less active. One or more of a dog's senses deteriorates and, as in humans, minor (or major) symptoms such as joint pain occur. Some very old dogs neglect their personal grooming and therefore require much more attention from their owners. Others start acting a bit strangely. Of course, chronic and serious illnesses can also occur and this is something that every dog owner should look out for.

With proper medical intervention, some of these illnesses will not negatively affect, or affect only a little, a dog's quality of life. Others can prove to be a great burden for both owner and animal. Despite this, many aged dogs want to be active. They want to take part in the life of their family and contribute to it as best they can, even if it is doing something as simple as chasing the mailman down the path—each and every day.

According to current thinking, a dog's life can be divided into three stages: youth, adult and senior. However, the way in which a dog develops over the course of a lifetime is a complex process and not even scientists can agree on a single definition of aging. One can, for example, differentiate between the following phases of life: growth, reproduction, the beginning of the first signs of aging without any serious effects, and extreme old age. Some definitions divide life after the active reproductive phase is over into three stages. However, this categorization applies more to human beings than to dogs since, compared to us, dogs remain much longer in the reproductive phase. But it is certain that the aging process starts off gradually. Only later, as a result of this process, do signs of aging begin to appear.

"Aging is a physiological change to the body that occurs later in life."

THE AGING PROCESS—
what happens to mind & body?

Every dog owner notices changes in his or her four-legged friend as it ages. The first sign is usually the appearance of gray fur on its muzzle, which, over the years, spreads further and further.

Gray hairs on a dog's face are often the first external signs that it is aging.

Most senior dogs also lose muscle mass, which is replaced by fairly large fat deposits. At the same time, a dog's tolerance for stress diminishes and it will need to sleep more.

These unmistakable external signs of aging are preceded by complex processes in the body. Yet even today, when numerous genomes have been decoded, the aging process presents many riddles. There is even a special branch of research, biogerontology, which attempts to discover the causes of biological aging. Hundreds of theories have been developed on this topic; many have been discredited, some have achieved general acceptance. But, all researchers are of the same opinion on one point: the aging process has its origins in the body's smallest reactors—the cells.

Some theories concentrate on general wear and tear to the body. As a rule, this means the deterioration of tissue and bones, which results in illness when a certain level of wear and tear has been reached. In contrast to this purely mechanical process, there is also the deterioration of cells to consider, which is a kind of "chemical erosion." During the metabolic process, which occurs in cells when food and oxygen are turned into energy, thousands of so-called free radicals are created every day along with other molecules. These free-radical molecules damage the body's cells by attacking their DNA. In fact, though, cells have numerous defense strategies to combat this kind of damage and ways of repairing themselves. Antioxidants such as vitamin C and vitamin E, zinc, and selenium play an important role. But, at some point, a cell's ability to regenerate becomes exhausted and the cell becomes weaker and, finally, dies.

Other theories have at their core the idea that old age is genetically pre-programmed. In a healthy adult, most cells split in two so that a younger copy of the original cell can continue to perform the cell's function. During this division process, a small piece at the end of the cell's DNA chain is lost. If the lost piece contained crucial genetic information, errors are made as the new cell goes about its tasks, and the cell dies off. The fewer the number

Q WHY DOES A DOG'S MUZZLE GO GRAY ?

A Hair root cells produce the pigment melanin, which gives hair its color. As a result of the aging process, these hair root cells are damaged and melanin production is stopped. The greater the number of cells there are that have stopped producing melanin, the whiter a dog's muzzle is. And, when there are pigment disorders or scars, even young dogs can get white hairs in these areas. Dogs who have dark hair on their faces often look older than they are, even though they are fairly young, since the gray hairs show up more on them than on dogs with a lighter coat.

Q IS THERE AN AGING GENE?

A Announcements are always floating around in the press about the existence of an "aging gene." But according to current scientific thought there is no one single gene that determines how long an organism will live. However, genes play an important role in how a body's cells protect themselves against damage and how they repair any damage. It is important to remember that both physical and mental stress cause cell damage and can lead to your dog's aging ahead of its time.

of cells that are left to maintain body functions, the sooner typical signs of aging will appear. Scientists call this pre-set number of possible cell divisions "programmed cell death" (apoptosis). It was also discovered that a cell's ability to divide is dependent on an organism's age. Cells of healthy younger organisms divide more often than those of older ones.

With increasing age, nerve cell loss occurs and brain function declines. This results in a reduced ability to react to new routines or situations, for example. An example of this is the stubbornness demonstrated by some senior dogs. Depending on the degree of age-related damage, senile dementia can also occur. This means older dogs find learning new things much more difficult since connections between nerve cells are not made as easily as in younger years. Connections that already exist break down and the dog reacts much more slowly to new stimulation. They might not remember where they are after waking up from a nap, for example. On the other hand, knowledge that has been already acquired, such as obeying commands, often can be reliably tapped. This in part balances out many of the dog's failing abilities and functions. It should not be too surprising to learn that a senior dog is capable of adjusting to new surroundings or is able to learn new things, just usually at a slower pace. After all, one would never dare to suggest that an older human being is incapable of adapting to new situations, even when it takes longer to do so than might have been the case in earlier years.

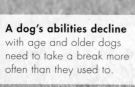

A dog's abilities decline with age and older dogs need to take a break more often than they used to.

THE BIOLOGICAL CLOCK

There is physical age, but there is also biological age. A fit person can be up to ten years younger biologically than his or her physical age. In dogs, this can make a difference of one or two years.

Of course, the opposite is also true; the body can also be biologically older than it actually is in years. More and more scientists have come to the conclusion that various factors play a role in the aging process. These have an influence on one another and comprise important elements of various current theories about aging. Environmental toxins cause cell damage, for example, and can lead to their death or degeneration. This can pave the way for future illnesses.Vitamins, hormones, and the body's hormone balance play an important role in slowing down the biological clock and improving the quality of life in old age. Damaging factors such as stress and free radicals must be held in check as much as possible. The kind of care a dog enjoys, such as the type of food it is fed and how well its owner maintains its physical and mental fitness, has a huge influence on how well a dog ages. Proper dog care is a simple and inexpensive way of helping to keep your dog fit for a long time.

Q IS IT TRUE THAT A DOG HAS A HIGHER LIFE EXPECTANCY WHEN ITS ANCESTORS LIVED TO A RIPE OLD AGE?

A Yes, the probability is quite high that their descendants will live longer. Most likely the dog's ancestors had good cell-defense mechanisms that protected their cells and repaired them after exposure to damaging influences. It is to be hoped that they have passed on these qualities to their offspring. In contrast, errors in the DNA and poor protective mechanisms can lead to premature aging and death.

DOES A DOG YEAR
equal seven human years?

In order to get an idea about what a dog is still capable of doing, and what its health status might be, many dog owners find it helpful to make a comparison between dog age and human age.

Almost everyone has heard the rule-of-thumb that one year in the life of a dog is equal to seven years in the life of a human being. Even when this rough guideline provides some sort of point-of-reference for dogs that are old, it is much more difficult and complex than this to compare human age with dog age. Many charts have been drawn up that make an attempt at comparison. However, even

A life on the run
A dog's life is over more quickly than that of a human's but this does not mean it is less satisfying.

when results seem similar, the charts' authors arrive at different conclusions. One has to remember that dogs age differently to human beings, and size, as well as genetic predisposition and illness, plays a large role in the way they age. Small and medium-sized breeds are fully grown at about one year of age. By contrast, a human being is still a child at seven years of age. Dogs are able to reproduce at one year of age, although this isn't recommended, and at this age are more similar to teenagers between 15 and 17 years old. A two-year-old dog is about the same age as a 25-year-old person. You can add about five to seven years for each year after this.

"Different-sized dogs have different life expectancies."

In making this kind of comparison, you have to take into account that different-sized dogs have different life expectancies. Large dogs, such as Great Danes, grow more quickly, remain childish longer, and are often slow to become mature. Small dogs, such as Miniature Poodles, usually live longer than large breeds and this is best seen in a chart (*see below*).

AGE COMPARISONS BETWEEN HUMANS AND DOGS (Estimates)

	DOG YEARS	1	3	5	8	10	12	15	18
Small	to 31lb (14kg)	18	28	38	53	63	73	88	103
Medium	33lb–60lb (15kg–30kg)	16	29	40	55	64	77	95	115
Large	60lb–99lb (30kg–45kg	15	30	45	66	81	96	117	
Very large	over 99lb (45kg)	14	32	48	76	94	110		

HUMAN YEARS

HUMAN YEARS

Differences in aging
Placing the age of a dog in relation to that of a human being on a chart can only provide a rough comparison.

BREED TYPES
& life expectancy

The life expectancy of dogs has increased just as it has for human beings. There are many reasons for this.

One reason is that dogs today are generally fed well-balanced diets; another is that dogs today live in much safer environments. In the past, many dogs ate poorly and worked at dangerous or difficult jobs that often resulted in injuries and early wear and tear. And, in the fields of preventive medicine and the treatment of illnesses, medical care has become much better than it once was. In the past, a serious illness was often a death sentence for a dog since its owner was not prepared to invest time and money in an aged or sick dog. Today it goes without saying for most people that their canine companions receive, as much as possible, the kind of medical care that their owners themselves would like to receive.

As a general rule one can say that smaller dogs live longer than larger dogs and that there are significant differences between breeds as to life expectancy. Miniature poodles, for example, often live to age 15 whereas this would be a biblical age for a Great Dane or an Irish Wolfhound. Dogs belonging to large breeds have the lowest life expectancy and usually live to about 6 or 8 years since the probability of heart disease and bone cancer is higher for them than it is for smaller dogs. Looking at all types of dogs, the average life expectancy is about 12 years. But even within the same breed there are large differences in the life expectancy of the dogs. This is due to a variety of genetic factors. For this reason, when you are thinking about acquiring a puppy, it is a good idea to see its parents and grandparents when possible. Some purebred dogs are famous for their longevity and breeders show these senior dogs with pride. Large purebred dogs are considered old when they are 6 years old, medium-sized dogs when they are 8, and small dogs when they are 10. Whether or not a dog truly feels old and behaves accordingly depends on its biological age.

It pays to cast a critical eye on very popular breeds and to make sure you acquire your puppy from a serious breeder. Popular purebred dogs often are churned out in puppy mills under terrible conditions to make money quickly for their breeders. No note is taken whether or not the parent dogs are healthy and free of genetic disease, something serious breeders check into as a matter of course. Many dogs bred in puppy mills are frequent and

A DOG TALE

When I acquired Lena, my female Ibizan Podenco, from Spain, I was told she was between three and four years old. Since she was in excellent condition, and her teeth were in great shape, my veterinarian did not have any reason to doubt this information. However, in the course of our life together, more and more typical signs of aging appeared. Her face became very "dry," she lost muscle mass and turned snow-white. Since now I am better able to compare other young and old dogs belonging to this breed, I am now certain that when Lena moved in she was at least eight years old. This goes to show that a single photograph does not always give enough reliable information about a dog's age!

A DOG TALE

Even when he was quite old my Afghan Hound Nicky loved to initiate wild games of chase with his friend Shalim, who was six years younger that he was. The older he grew, the shorter the chases, but he was always completely engaged in the game. When his energy flagged, he simply lay down for a little break. Then, in a flash, the game started up again. He could always judge when he had taken on too much.

life-long visitors to veterinarians and often die at a relatively young age. Ask your veterinarian for recommendations, speak with people who own the kind of breed you are interested in acquiring, and check with animal rescue organizations to get further information about a given breed and puppy mills in your area.

Some purebred dogs are more likely to contract certain types of diseases due to genetic predisposition—sometimes several all at the same time. As a result, these animals have a reduced life-expectancy. In general, mongrels are considered to be healthier than purebreds. This is due to their genetic variety since they carry the genes of at least two breeds. However, often one does not know which hereditary factors have been passed on to a mixed breed dog. In the best possible case, a dog will inherit all the positive characteristics of its ancestors, but it can also suffer from inherited medical problems or, as a carrier, pass these on to its descendents.

In the long run, everything depends on the hand nature has dealt the dog; the genetic outcome is unpredictable. If the dog's parents are both purebred dogs with a predisposition to hip dysplasia, epilepsy, heart disease, or blindness, to name just a few diseases, there is a high probability that their offspring will also contract these diseases or pass them on to their descendants. And, just as unlikely as it is that dogs with noble pedigrees are immune to infections and general illnesses, it is unlikely that mutts are also immune, even when they are so charming and special.

WHY ARE OLD DOGS
so special?

"Daily events, routines and habits provide security."

Throughout the many years they have spent together, dog and man grow close and turn into a close-knit team. They have come to know one another intimately over time.

They can instantly size each other up and interpret each other's gestures and expressions. Just a quick glance into a dog's eyes tells its human whether the dog is feeling uncomfortable or not. Small, almost insignificant, details forewarn the senior dog about various events and developments in the family. Daily routines and habits of family members have become transparent to the dog. It often knows ahead of time that a walk is in the offing or that its human is getting ready to go out to a party.

Even senior dogs
can tear loose and be foolish, play, and frolic about just like their youthful counterparts.

Whether you have decided to take a walk with your dog or you are just going down the block to the supermarket, you do not need to tell your dog what you are planning. It will know what is happening by the shoes you choose. Sometimes it even seems to know what you are going to do when you simply think about doing it. This is especially noticeable when vacation preparations are underway. Many dogs never let packed suitcases out of their sight so that they will not be forgotten, or they take every opportunity to jump into the car. On a daily basis, your canine companion knows when it has to stay home and probably does not even bother getting up to go to the door ahead of you—your schedule is its schedule. Daily events, routine, habits—these are words that are usually considered negative. But, for a family, and for dogs, these things certainly provide security.

Experience a senior dog has gathered throughout its life has left its mark on it and made it wise. It rarely does something without thinking or without reason. Its knowledge about the daily routines of the family, or its immediate environment, allow it to size up situations correctly. While it might have senselessly chased every crow it saw in its youth, today, at the most, it will simply raise its eyebrow for an instant as if to say "interesting, but absolutely unobtainable." Many dogs achieve this kind of wisdom only when they are quite advanced in age. But still, even older dogs can sometimes tear around, act silly and seem to be much younger than they are. Due perhaps to failing senses, some older dogs are unable properly to size up danger as they once could. When this happens, people have to watch over their dogs much more carefully so that they do not end up in prickly situations.

Whatever kind of life a person leads with an elderly dog, whether it is characterized by calmness, harmony and balance, or is centered around worry for an ailing dog, the lives of dog and human are entwined with each other through the many years they have spent together.

A DOG TALE

Two years ago, my ten-year-old Afghan Hound Shalim came down with a serious, life-threatening illness and needed around-the-clock care. It was months before he recovered fully—then he broke his foot! But now he is good as new, seems to be even more full of beans than ever, and is in fantastic condition for his age. Even if your dog is old, intensive care pays off.

DAILY LIFE WITH A SENIOR DOG

THERE IS NO PATENT RECIPE for dealing with an elderly dog. Whether or not your senior companion's behavior and physical constitution changes as it grows old age, and to what degree, varies from animal to animal. An aging dog's daily routine might not have to be altered at all, just a little, or perhaps more radically.

As long as there are no underlying health problems, day-to-day life with a senior dog is generally more relaxed and stress-free than it is at the side of a lively and adventurous youngster. Man and dog are a coordinated team—each knows what to expect from the other. A routine has been established, both at home and when undertaking joint activities, that makes life easier for all participants. Many aged dogs take part in their family's activities with great pleasure, and are perfectly happy to go on longer trips. However, they also enjoy—and need—restful and cozy days at home. As a caring dog owner, you take all your dog's requirements into account and create a comfortable environment for it as best you can. This can sometimes mean overcoming quite a few challenges when your dog has already reached old age or is suffering from a serious illness. In such cases organizational talent—among other things—is needed to cater for the needs of both two-legged and four-legged animals.

DAILY ROUTINE

Inner clock
Old dogs know the daily routine. They always know when it is chow time.

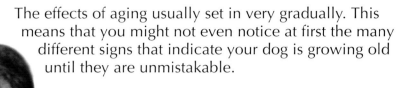

The effects of aging usually set in very gradually. This means that you might not even notice at first the many different signs that indicate your dog is growing old until they are unmistakable.

Day by day, you will grow into the responsibilities that arise when caring for a senior dog. Gradually, they will become part of the daily routine. However, when a dog becomes ill, greater adjustments might well be called for. Try not to see this as a problem but as a challenge, one that can be readily mastered. By using your imagination, being extremely well organized each day, choosing good tools to help you out and securing the help of kind people, you will rise to the occasion.

ROUTINE

Accustomed routine and ritualized activities give a senior dog security and help foster a trusting relationship between it and humans. Being able to implicitly trust the person at its side is essential for a dog's well-being. Without this, it will not be able to enjoy successful social relationships with other dogs (see p88). For senior dogs in particular, having a predictable daily routine is extremely important.

By following a constant daily routine when you feed your dog and take it for walks you gain several advantages even above and beyond simply giving a structure to the day. Many older dogs' digestion is affected by even small disruptions to routine. Unaccustomed food and changed feeding times can lead to diarrhea, constipation, gas, or loss of appetite. By arranging your schedule so your dog is fed daily within the same two-hour time slot, you can usually keep to your daily dog-walking rhythm. If you vary these set times too much, your dog will, of course, need to relieve itself at different times than it is accustomed to and you will have to walk it more often so that it can completely empty its bladder. No matter what their age, all dogs should rest for two hours after eating before being allowed to run around or play. Set feeding times are also very important when you have to give your dog medications at precise times (see p129). Since these times will vary (for example, before eating or with food), keeping a regular routine is not only helpful, it is absolutely necessary. It will also help you remember to give your dog the right medication at the right time.

A DOG TALE

It was very hard for my eleven-year-old Ibizan Podenco female Lena to handle disruptions to her routine. Whenever we spent a weekend visiting friends she found it very tiring. Given the slightest alteration to her routine she stopped eating or did not even make an attempt to eat. Since Lena needed heart medication twice a day, her refusal to eat was a real problem for me. Giving a dog pills on an empty stomach is not ideal.

Back at home in her accustomed environment, Lena often needed two days of complete peace and quiet to recover from the weekend away and slept most of this time. We rarely undertook long excursions during Lena's last year of life in order to reduce the stress that both human and dog experienced.

WALKS

It is extremely important for a dog, no matter how old it is, to be taken on regular walks. Walks fulfill many needs. Foremost is the dog's need for adequate physical exercise. Exercise animates its cardiovascular system, improving its blood supply and ensuring a good oxygen supply. Strong muscles help support and hold together joints and spine. After all, there is sound reasoning behind the age-old saying "Those who rest, rust!" When you are walking your dog, it is important to be able to judge correctly how much your dog can and cannot do so as not to under- or overtax it (*see p76*). Always keep in mind any health limitations your dog has. Make sure your dog gets regular, varied, physical activity well into old age; this is essential to its well-being. Since quite a few senior dogs relish their comfort above all, you will also need to come up with really good ideas to tempt them off the sofa.

A DOG TALE

My two eleven-year-old Staffordshire Terriers have very different personalities. When Tony first opens his eyes in the morning he's in a fantastic mood whereas Daisy is quite grumpy. It's almost as though she needs a strong cup of coffee to wake up properly. Their differences are also very obvious during walks: Tony happily runs ahead, Daisy lags behind, and I walk in the middle. After all, I'm the one that has to slow down one animal and encourage the other to move along.

Walks
give structure to the day. Senior dogs should be taken on many short walks rather than few long walks.

Sniffing along the edges of paths teaches a dog almost everything about its immediate surroundings and trains all its senses.

Nosing around

On the daily rounds you walk with your dog it exercises all its senses. As it sniffs thoroughly along a path's edge, your dog is finding out which dog went by and left its mark, where, and when. To a dog, this is almost like reading a newspaper. Smell is a dog's most developed sense, and identifying scents stimulates its brain enormously. In order to maintain a dog's mental fitness as long as possible, its senses have to be stimulated as often as possible. For this reason, it is not good enough to let your dog exercise solely within the confines of its own garden, especially since a dog moves about much less in familiar territory than in fields and woods.

Not every senior dog still enjoys horsing around but meeting other dogs is very important.

Meeting friends

To a dog, going on a walk also means meeting others of its kind, taking care of social contacts, making new contacts, and communicating extensively. Of course, as dogs grow older, the amount of time they spend racing around and playing, and the intensity of these activities, declines more and more. Despite this, older dogs should not be kept in isolation. They should be given the opportunity of meeting other dogs on a daily basis since this benefits them enormously.

Individual needs

There are many senior dogs that accompany their owners on long walks with great stamina and enormous pleasure. Others still have kept up their enthusiasm for sports. Effortlessly, they are able to keep up the pace, happily running alongside their two-legged companions as they cycle, inline skate, or jog. The kind of activity you can expect of your dog depends on its physical condition (*see p74*).

If your dog is very old, you might have to take it on more frequent but shorter walks every day due, for example, to its lack of endurance or joint problems (*see p77*). Also, aged dogs might need to urinate or defecate more often. If this is the case, you should give your dog the opportunity to relieve itself in the garden or on the front lawn as often as needed between regular walks—even at night.

Running at a steady pace alongside a bicycle strengthens a dog's muscles, heart, and respiratory system. If it has joint problems, let your senior dog run on soft surfaces rather than paved roads.

"The kind of activity you can expect of your dog depends on its physical condition."

A DOG TALE

Kira, my Labrador Retriever bitch is eleven years old and still loves going on walks even in deepest winter. She also adores swimming in the lake. After a chilly dip, I have to make sure she keeps moving so she doesn't cool down and catch a cold.

Summertime

Check out the weather forecast before taking your dog out for its daily walks. When temperatures are high, plan longer walks for the early morning or late evening hours. Around noontime, just take a short walk, ideally in a shady forest or a park. If your dog is an enthusiastic swimmer, it will enjoy a refreshing dip in a stream or lake, even into ripe old age (*see p78*). Always remember to take drinking water along with you when it is hot outside so that your dog can quench its thirst underway.

The right path

Healthy dogs can be taken for walks anywhere. But, if your dog has joint or spine problems, you should keep it off hard surfaces such as asphalt or concrete. Walking on hard surfaces compresses a dog's joints and disks. As a dog ages, this can aggravate existing problems, or even cause them (*see p75*). Good alternatives are paths with soft surfaces such as are found in forests, fields and meadows, and on sandy soil. On hot, sunny days, another advantage is that your dog's paws will not be burned on soft-surfaced paths as they might be on asphalt or concrete ones.

Calm through experience
Even during a stroll in a meadow dotted with curious cows, this elderly female Boxer remains calm.

STAYING ALONE

The way an elderly dog behaves when it stays alone at home depends primarily on how well it has adjusted to being alone in the past. If a dog is used to spending several hours in a row without its human companions on a regular basis, or even being alone every now and then, then there usually will not be any problems as the dog ages. Elderly dogs that have never experienced staying at home without their pack can be trained to do so. However, the training is not always successful.

"I'm waiting for you."
Many older dogs enjoy having some time all to themselves.

Things can change

Of course, as they age, some dogs attach themselves even more closely to their humans. They become more dependent, and find it very difficult to be separated from them. Even a change to a dog's environment, a move, or a family member's leaving home, for example, can trigger a change in its behavior. The presence of a second dog in a home, one that is self-confident, can give such dogs a sense of security and relieve their anxiety.

On no account will a dog's separation anxiety resolve itself with age. Intensive training as well as a great deal of patience and understanding is required in order to control, if at all possible, a dog's fear.

If a dog becomes increasingly restless or uncertain, the causes can be illnesses such as various cardiovascular diseases (*see p140*), or age-related dementia. Whenever your senior dog suddenly exhibits different behavior from normal, describe your observations to your veterinarian and talk to a good dog trainer to see what the best course of action is.

However, sometimes it can also happen that the behavior of old dogs that used to be unhappy when their owners were absent changes. Now they are older, they need more rest, and so gladly spend the time alone napping.

Q DO I NEED TO PUT A BLANKET OR A COAT ON MY TEN-YEAR-OLD DOG IN WINTER?

A Young and active dogs do not need warm coverings in winter. The same is true for most elderly dogs. Putting coats or blankets on dogs to protect them from the cold is superfluous. It is more important to keep senior dogs moving so they do not get cold. However, when older dogs are suffering from arthritis, or joint or spine problems, you might want to cover them up since their symptoms can be exacerbated by cold, especially damp cold. Also, older dogs that readily feel the cold because they have short hair, or little or no undercoat, appreciate a warm covering when it is cold or raining heavily outside. However, before you swaddle your dog up like a little mummy, or dress it up in an outfit, you should ask your veterinarian whether or not this is really necessary.

If your dog really needs a warm coat, choose one first for its functionality, then for the way it looks. When a dog coat fits badly—if it slips, constrains the dog or pinches it in any way—the animal will move less and then it will definitely freeze.

Part-time job for a senior
Most dogs enjoy going to work every-day with their owners. Sometimes, though, taking a break and getting some rest is more important.

"Leave the dog sitter with a telephone number where you can be reached at all times."

Taking your dog to work

Today, more and more employers are allowing their employees to bring their dogs to work. In fact, studies have proven that, in most cases, bringing dogs to work has a positive effect on the work climate. Dogs love it too! They love being with their masters or mistresses around the clock. And they find it very interesting to meet all those nice two-legged folk that people a work-place and every now and then give them extra pats and tasty treats.

When a dog is brought into your workplace it encounters a wide range of new impressions. These can be strange smells and sounds or simply being spoken to by colleagues—both known and unknown. This ensures variety and stimulation of its little gray cells.

As dogs age, they need more rest. In fact, many sleep so soundly that they are hard to wake up from their dreams even at the workplace. But if your dog startles up every time a colleague enters the room or the telephone rings, then spending the entire day in the office can be very tiring for it—it cannot get the rest that it requires. In such cases, it would be better to take your senior dog along to work only every second or third workday, and allow it to relax at home on the other days.

Dog care

No matter whether your dog remains at home alone or comes to work with you as part of the daily routine, you always have to have several alternative options for having your senior dog cared for or boarded. After all, a dog can become ill at any time, which will cause all the usual routines to change. Especially after surgery, dogs need a great deal of rest and care. Sometimes they cannot be left alone for several days. You also need to plan in advance for contingencies such as if you are unable to take care of your dog because of a business trip or you become ill. Try to prepare ahead for such situations because the right kind of planning will let you master them. Work out with family members, friends, and neighbors how your dog will be taken care of, if, due to the kind of job you have, you cannot do this yourself during the day or are unable to take off a few days of work at short notice. Perhaps you can come to an arrangement with another dog owner and take care of each other's dog as the situation requires?

If there is absolutely no one in your circle of friends and acquaintances to help you care for your dog, then dog sitters are always available. Dog sitters care for dogs in their accustomed environments or care for them in their own homes. To find a reliable one, first ask other dog owners who live in your area for recommendations and what their experience has been. Your veterinarian might also have some good suggestions. You can also find names and contact information for dog sitters in daily newspapers or specialist magazines, or on the Internet. Another care alternative is a good dog kennel (*see p46*). However, especially during or after a serious illness or operation a dog should be cared for in a trusted environment and by people it knows well.

Dog sitters

One should be aware that it is asking a lot of a dog sitter to care for an old or ailing dog. Discuss with your dog sitter what should happen in case of an emergency. This is essential, just as it is when a dog is healthy. It is also important to set down written instructions for the dog sitter or for anyone who takes care of your dog. Also, a written statement that allows the sitter to act in your dog's best interests in your absence can be invaluable when a veterinarian needs to be consulted. Note down everything that seems important to you,and make sure to leave a telephone number where you can be reached at all times.

In the best of company
When your aging dog is in the hands a good dog sitter you know your loyal friend is being well taken care of.

Taking care of a dog
is a big responsibility. You have to be able to trust the dog sitter completely.

SENIOR DOGS & CHILDREN

A DOG TALE

Our daughters Theresa (twelve years old) and Johanna (eleven years) grew up with our two Pulis, Janosch and Kosko. Janosch is now ten years old and suffers from back problems. Ever since this was diagnosed, our children have been especially considerate toward him. For example, they always carry him up and down the stairs in their arms and they no longer play with him as wildly as before. Our girls even tell us off when, by accident, we occasionally let him walk on stairs. Children, too, are capable of behaving considerately.

Dogs are very special companions for children. A child can entrust all of his important secrets to its four-legged friend without reservation, and share every happy or sad experience with it. A dog gives comfort and is a patient listener that tells no tales.

Friendship with a dog is something very special and gives a child a feeling of security and safety. Very often, a child's relationship with the very first dog he or she lives with will remain a treasured memory throughout life and play an important role in his or her childhood development.

LIFELONG LEARNING

Living day to day with a dog in the family improves a child's social competence. He has to recognize a dog's needs, respond to its facial expressions and movements and communicate wordlessly with the animal. This promotes and trains good observation skills and understanding. A child learns to show consideration for a dog and how to take care of its daily needs. Feeding it, caring for it, or taking it on walks—even when the child would much rather be playing with friends at the time, or the weather is inclement—decidedly influences emotional development and has a positive effect on many other areas of the child's life.

Together through thick and thin
The experience of growing up with a four-legged friend enriches a child's life and also helps it learn how to follow rules.

PARENTAL RESPONSIBILITIES

Depending on their age and maturity, children can take over some of a dog's care with proper instruction and supervision. However, they are not able to take on the responsibility for the total care of a dog—this always remains a parent's task. She or he must ensure that the needs of the dog are met, even when the child wants to pursue other interests. The parents make decisions, assess a given situation and its risks, draw up the rules, and set limits.

Parents must ensure
that the needs of both child and dog are met and that neither comes to harm.

RULES FOR CHILDREN

→ Do not disturb the dog when it is eating

→ Do not disturb the dog when it is sleeping

→ Do not stare at the dog

→ Do not pet the dog without first talking to it

→ Do not pet the dog when it does not want to be petted

→ Do not pinch, push, or ram the dog

→ Do not pull on the dog's ears, tail, or fur

→ Do not take away a dog's food or toys

→ Stand still and look away when a dog becomes too wild

→ Turn your body away and look in another direction when the dog growls

→ Only play with the dog when adults are present

→ Do not touch strange dogs without first asking permission of the dog's owner and your parents

→ Stand still and look away when a dog that is unknown to you comes along

Clear rules

As the dominant human, it is your job to define clearly who is in charge and which actions overstep the boundaries you have set. The latter is valid for both dog and child! Children have to learn the correct way of behaving around a dog. This is also important for their own safety. Every dog needs to be able to retreat and to sleep without disturbance. Very old dogs are more apt to startle easily because their senses are failing and might react unpredictably if surprised. When your senior dog is resting or sleeping, it should be off-limits to children and visitors alike.

Great care must be exercised when a child and senior dog are engaged in wild horseplay, especially when the dog is suffering from pain. This pain can be caused by a chronic illness or another health problem such as deterioration of the joints or spine. If the dog is touched unthinkingly or clumsily, it might react defensively and, possibly, bite. Therefore, when a dog is suffering from an acute illness that is accompanied by constant pain it might even be a good idea to prevent all close contact between a child and dog until the dog has fully recovered or definitely is on the mend.

Dog toys should always be strictly off-limits to children.

Visiting children

Especially children who grew up without animals in the house can be either very forward or very fearful in the presence of dogs. They often react surprisingly—running away from the dog in fear or wildly waving their arms about. This can escalate the situation. What a dog allows "its" children to do is not tolerated for long from strange children.

However, even visiting children who are already living with or used to dogs do not always strike the right balance. Sometimes they expect too much of a four-legged playmate. As parents, you must keep track of what is happening and be able to intervene so that a dog does not feel cornered and a child is not endangered. Sometimes it is better to allow the dog its needed rest in another room in order to prevent conflicts before they arise. As a rule, you should never leave children and dogs unsupervised.

This old female dog
calmly accepts a demonstration of affection from her little friend. Dogs do not always submit to such closeness. If this is the case—watch out!

Strange encounters
Children and dogs should never be allowed to get near each other without supervision.

A NEW "SENIOR" AND CHILDREN

If you take in an older dog that is unaccustomed to children, and your offspring have never lived with a four-legged friend, then there is a great deal to learn on both sides. From the very beginning it must be made absolutely clear to the senior dog that the family's children outrank it. At the very least, it should learn to behave neutrally toward them. Dogs consider small children to be playmates and therefore do not acknowledge them as leaders. It is only when children reach puberty that their status can change. However, they do not automatically assume a dominant role. Sometimes even 20-year olds still are treated as children by their parents and so, to a dog, they remain at the same level too.

A NEW BABY

If your dog has grown old in your household and behaves, at the least, neutrally toward children, then you should not expect to experience any great problems with your canine friend when a little one suddenly arrives. Exceptions are dogs that are uncomfortable in the presence of children or those that behave aggressively toward them. And too, dogs that have enjoyed being the focal point of a family might attempt to maintain this central role by exhibiting undesirable behavior. If you do not know how your dog will relate to a baby, you should, as early as possible, hire a good dog trainer to evaluate it. Use the gestation period to prepare

This four-legged companion is always in control of a situation, watching out to ensure that nothing happens to its young ones.

your four-legged friend for the infant's arrival with the help of the trainer. In any case, it is a good idea to refresh a dog's basic obedience training at this time so that you can better handle it once the baby has arrived. Daily life is made much easier when a dog obeys sit, stay, or go commands consistently and unhesitatingly. The time that you invest in your dog now will pay for itself many times over when the baby has arrived. But, if your dog behaves in an unexpected way toward your baby do not wait—call your trainer immediately.

"Dogs consider small children to be playmates."

Involving the dog

There are many and varied opinions as to how to get a dog and a baby used to each other. In the cases we are aware of, the dogs were involved in everything from the very beginning, which worked extremely well. Do not isolate your dog. Let him participate in everyday life. Bring home items such as baby powder and other baby care products early enough so that your dog can get used to their scents. Place clothing that your baby has worn in the hospital in your dog's basket before the baby's arrival. When you come

Please play with me!
Despite the fuss over a new baby, you should always find time to spend with your four-legged friend so that it does not feel rejected and then reacts in ways you will not approve of.

home from the hospital, try to arrange it so you enter the house with both dog and baby at the same time. Let your four-legged friend smell the baby and make physical contact with it. Make sure, though, that your dog does not always push its way into the center of the action. Even canine mothers decide for themselves whether or not other dogs, even trusted ones, are allowed to come into contact with their puppies early on. Sometimes they let several weeks go by before they allow other dogs near their offspring. It can also happen that an older dog has, at first, absolutely no interest in the baby. There also are very curious dogs that immediately come over to look at and thoroughly sniff over a new baby. Luckily, dogs realize very quickly that the baby is part of the immediate family. Perhaps you even will have to curb your dog's protective behavior somewhat so that strangers are able to take a little peek into the baby carriage.

From the very first day you come home with your new baby, let your dog know unmistakably what kinds of behavior you consider appropriate and what you will not accept. Express disapproval by completely ignoring it, for example, when you think your dog is overreacting (*see p91*). By properly managing its behavior from the start, you will not have to keep correcting it—or even punishing it—later on.

Once a day, at the very least, you should devote some quality time to your dog. Play with it, give it jobs to do, or have it perform exercises it learned in a training program. Free up some time for this activity. Spending time with your dog will help ensure that it does not sink out of sight in the general fuss over the baby, does not feel rejected, and does not vie for attention with inappropriate behavior.

HYGIENE

There are some rules of hygiene that should be followed when dogs and children come into contact with each other. For example, it is important to vaccinate and worm the dog regularly after consulting your veterinarian (*see p125*). It is almost impossible to prevent close physical contact between dogs and children. Dogs are always more than ready to lick cake crumbs off a child's hands, and many a child's face has been "cleaned" by a rough dog tongue. Such close contact should not lead to "hygiene hysteria"—this is uncalled for. It has been proven scientifically that exposure to germs in fact strengthens the immune system, and that excessive elimination of germs is actually very counterproductive! It is usually sufficient to teach children always to wash their hands after coming in contact with a dog.

Rules of hygiene do not just serve to protect your child, but also to protect your dog. People probably pass on more infections to dogs than dogs do to people. For example, you can readily pass on an influenza virus or a tonsil infection to your dog. Therefore, if you or your child's nose is running or you are plagued by a cough, try to avoid coming into close physical contact with your dog, especially if it is very old or chronically ill and its immune system is compromised.

SENIOR DOGS
& other dogs

Dogs are a pack animals and usually feel comfortable in family clans or groups. Human beings cannot replace the social contact and communication a dog needs to have with other members of its species.

If you have only one dog living with you, give it regular opportunities of socializing with other dogs. Not even an old dog likes being isolated, and interacting with other dogs brings variety into its daily routine.

When they are old, some wild bachelor dogs or cheeky alpha-males become calmer and more relaxed in the company of other dogs. The experience a dog has gained over the years enables it to react in a wiser and more tempered way. It no longer has to prove itself continually and its behavior is more restrained. However, it is unlikely that a canine companion will change its tune if it has already shown a pattern of bad behavior toward other members of its species while on the leash.

A wet demonstration
of affection is not unhygienic. Just wash your hands afterward and everything will be clean again.

Together with other dogs
dogs can experience adventures that their owners never can offer them, even when they try their best.

"One cannot let every dog off the leash so that it can socialize."

Sometimes, for health reasons, it can also happen that dogs that once were confident and calm become uncertain and more hesitant. Showing sympathy is the wrong reaction. It is better to behave neutrally in such cases. Your four-legged companion will take its cues from you if you convey certainty and authority in your body language. At the least, you will avoid reinforcing uncertain behavior. If you have recently opened up your home and heart to an older dog (*see p59ff.*), you will have to test it bit by bit to see how well it socializes with other dogs.

BE ALERT

Take care, especially if you have an aged dog, that it does not overexert itself when it is tearing around and playing with much younger members of its kind. If the situation demands it, intervene before your dog's energy is spent. Not all dogs pay heed to their own physical limitations. Also, when your dog is playing with dogs of different sizes, you should monitor them to prevent

Whenever possible, dogs should be able to socialize with each other when they are off-leash.

OFF-LEASH EXERCISE

Can you can let your senior dog off the leash? Then it is a good idea to allow social interaction between your dog and another dog when it is off the leash and free to perform all the rituals of social contact. First, before you allow the two animals near each another, talk to the other dog's owner. Ask whether or not a dog that is unfamiliar to you is well socialized and behaves properly toward other dogs. However, under no circumstances should you allow yourself to be coerced by other dog owners into letting your dog off the leash. Listen to your feelings and if either the other dog or the person who is accompanying it appears untrustworthy, forego the attempt.

ON THE LEASH

One cannot allow every dog off the leash so that it can socialize with other dogs. If you have taken in an older dog, then much time and effort might well be needed to train the dog before supervised off-leash exercise is feasible. Depending on the kinds of experiences your senior dog has had in the past, and what it learned or did not learn, it is entirely possible that it will only be able to run on an extendable leash or in a fenced-in area. Despite this, it is a good idea to practice letting your dog off-leash because even older dogs are very capable of learning new things (*see p85–91*).

The behavior of dogs that are on the leash and meeting other dogs can be very different from that exhibited when they are freed from the leash. Some dogs behave boorishly and cheekily. Specialists have many different explanations for this kind of behavior. For example, perhaps the leash, which is a direct link to its handler, makes the dog feel stronger. Perhaps, too, the dog is frustrated by restrictions to its movements or is feels insecure because there is no way of escaping or because greeting rituals common to dogs cannot be practiced. It also might be the case that the dog does not view the person at the end of the leash as being in control of the situation and sees itself, then, as having to play the role of protector.

A leash prevents a dog from behaving according to its nature and, therefore, is often a necessary security measure.

LEASHES FOR ALL OCCASIONS

Extending leashes and tow leashes allow a dog to move around with some freedom in places where off-leash exercise is not allowed. An extending leash is also ideal for off-leash training and a leather leash ideal in the city.

Extending leash

32ft (10m) tow leash

Leather leash

SENIOR DOGS
and other animals

Dogs are pack animals, and many are able to tolerate living with animals from other species. Exceptions are dogs with highly developed hunting instincts.

It is easier and less problematic later on to introduce dogs as puppies to other animals in the household. In most cases though, old or aged dogs also can be successfully integrated into your extended family.

DOGS AND CATS

Real friendships can develop between dogs and cats over the years. If an older dog moves in and a cat is already living with you, then, from the very outset, you must let your dog know that it is not allowed to chase the cat. To prevent this from happening, at least at the beginning, you should not leave the two animals alone and unsupervised. If your cat is accustomed to dogs, and can handle them, then it will most likely not run away but simply hold its ground by either sitting down on the spot or remaining standing. Cats also quickly learn that they can make good their escape from a rambunctious dog by climbing up onto furniture or a cat-tree. And too, many velvet-pawed felines are extremely self-confident. By hissing and through body language, cats let dogs know where the boundaries are.

Give these different animals time to adjust and do not force them into close contact with each other right away. Both your pets need to be allowed some distance before trust has been established and their relationship becomes more relaxed. Dogs and cats communicate in very different ways. At the beginning, this will be confusing to both species. And too, dogs and cats are creatures of habit and have to first learn to appreciate each other.

In the case of an older dog that has highly developed hunting instincts, one has to be very careful in getting it used to a cat. Since not every detail about an adopted dog's past is known, attempting to make a dog and cat live together in harmony might be a complete failure. If, over the course of years, a dog has considered cats as prey, as animals to be hounded, then it can be difficult, if not impossible, for the cat and dog ever to have an easy relationship. Unfortunately, any behavioral pattern that has been impressed onto a dog's brain over the years is very hard, if not impossible, to alter.

A DOG TALE

My Labrador Retriever, Kira, who is eleven years old, and Justus, who is eight, absolutely love our cats. They even protect them from other dogs. However, strange cats are always energetically chased off our property.

In my capacity as a veterinarian, I often took in orphaned baby squirrels or dormice and brought them home to raise. Usually, I transported them home in a cardboard box. Kira always participated enthusiastically in their upbringing. Whenever I left a box on a table or on the floor in the animal clinic, Kira watched over it eagerly in the hope that there was a little baby animal inside for her to take care of again. But I wouldn't rely on every dog to show this kind of affection toward other animals.

RABBITS, BIRDS, AND OTHER SMALL FRIENDS

There are dogs that lovingly cuddle, snuggle up against, and protect rabbits and other small animals and come to love them. However, only a small number of dogs show such friendly enthusiasm for these little beings.

As a rule, small animals such as rabbits, rodents, or birds should never be allowed to run around or fly freely inside a house since many dangers lurk in wait for them. This is especially true when a dog lives in the house. Even if your elderly dog ignores or seems to take no notice of the small pets, this is no guarantee of harmless coexistence. Fast or hectic movements can unleash the chase instinct that is part of every dog's nature.

You should also ensure that all cages or enclosures are securely fastened down and cannot be pulled over or opened. This is also important for outdoor cages, such as rabbit cages, and for outdoor enclosures. Also, dogs should not be able to harass caged animals whether it is by barking at them or banging their paws against their cages. Before your small mammals or birds come to harm, you should, as often as is called for, keep the dog away from them or even deny it any chance of getting near the cages. You should be especially observant when children are in the house. They will take the smaller animals out of their cages in order to play with them and forget all about the danger that can come from the dog.

These fowl have nothing to fear from this trusted canine since, to it, they are part-and-parcel of the household and farm.

THE RIGHT ENVIRONMENT

Dogs often have their own views about comfort. To us, this dog looks uncomfortable, but, to the dog, this is relaxation pure!

Senior dogs have special needs, depending on how fit they are. You can do a great deal to ensure that your trusted companion feels safe and secure, and that its living quarters are tailored to its special needs.

Offer your dog a comfortable home, one that takes into account any existing physical problems the may dog have. And too, the right living space design can help make your own daily life easier in countless ways when you have an elderly dog.

A DOG'S REFUGE

When a dog has reached a ripe old age it needs much more sleep than when it was young. You should make sure it has a comfortable sleeping and resting spot. This is its refuge, a place it can retreat to for a bit of peace and quiet when things become too much for it.

Just the right spot

By putting your dog's bed or basket in a central spot—such as the living room—you give it the opportunity to participate in family life. Even so, its bed should be a bit removed from the action, and protected by a corner or a wall. This ensures that people passing by, or opening and closing doors, do not wake up or scare the dog. It is less than ideal to place a dog's bed in the kitchen near the kitchen table or even under it, since many dogs will beg for their food there or feel that they have to defend their food. And too, a kitchen is a busy place. Some dogs have a tendency to want to dominate their humans and territory. Their beds should not be located in the hallway or in any spot where they can observe the entire apartment or the most important rooms in a house. This gives them even more self-confidence!

Types of beds

Pet stores offer a large selection of dog beds ranging from the old-fashioned standard—a Spartan blanket—to luxury designer items created with demanding and well-off dog owners in mind. When choosing your senior dog's bed, be guided by its needs and individual likes and dislikes. Important considerations to keep in mind are how comfortable is the bed and how easy will it be to keep clean?

A DOG TALE

To make my ten-year-old Retriever-mix Stanley as comfortable as possible, I bought him a dog bed filled with Styrofoam pellets. These adjust to a dog's form and, for this reason, are supposed to be very comfortable. As it turns out, my female dog, not Stanley, loves lying on this bed. Stanley makes a wide detour around it—the crackling noise made by the pellets spooks him. The next time I buy a dog bed I'll bring him along and let him try it out first!

Size

Many older dogs suffer from calluses on their joints caused by lying down on hard surfaces (*see p113*). A soft and roomy upholstered bed can help prevent them. For this reason, a dog's bed should be large enough that the dog can stretch out in it comfortably without bumping up against anything. A thick quilted blanket or a bed filled with Styrofoam pellets is ideal: a dog simply stretches its long legs out inside the bed or rests on its soft edges.

Hygiene

All textiles used by your dog should be washable at 140°F (60°C), at the very least, and be able to be dried in a clothes dryer. Ideally, beds and cushions should have removable covers. This is especially important for senior dogs that have problems controlling their bladders (*see p144*), since cushions and blankets will have to be cleaned daily. In such cases, waterproof covers made from fabrics such as imitation leather are practical. In case there is an accident, the filling will remain dry. Your canine friend is also well-bedded on a plushy microfiber blanket with a rubber undercoating. Textiles made of microfibers wick moisture away from a dog's body and ensure that it rests comfortably. This type of blanket also makes an excellent extra layer in the bed or can be thrown over the sofa to protect the upholstery.

DOG BEDS AND BASKETS

Baskets are difficult to keep clean.

Material-covered baskets wash easily.

A removable imitation leather cover is waterproof and easy to clean.

Plastic beds
are hygienic and, when a soft cushion is added, extremely cosy.

Individual climate control

If you set your dog's bed on a base that is 2 to 4 inches (5 to 10 centimeters) high, or on a thick piece of Styrofoam, you will keep your dog away from the cold floor, for which dogs with joint problems will be very grateful. But the bed should be raised no higher, especially for unsteady seniors, since this makes it hard for them to get in and out. Dogs that are still physically fit and take their proper place in the family hierarchy without a murmur of protest can certainly be allowed to lie on the sofa (*see p86–89*).

Older dogs that readily feel the cold often prefer a spot close to a heat source; some even wrap themselves completely up in their blankets until perhaps not even the tip of their noses peek out. These dogs are usually the smaller ones, and those with a sparse or no undercoat. Dogs with heavy coats often seek out a cooler spot to rest in, especially in summer. Their beds should not be placed too near a heat source. But they have their own preferences, so sometimes even a dog with a heavy coat appreciates a soft and warm bed.

A thick dog bed keeps away the cold floor and invites a dog to rest.

STAIRS

Many dogs that have spent their whole lives racing happily up and down stairs can still do so up until the time they die. Others might come to need some loving assistance from their humans.

Uncertainty

One reason a dog might have difficulty climbing stairs is uncertainty. Perhaps the dog slipped once on the stairs or it no longer recognizes individual steps due to failing vision.

Sometimes, in order to give a dog a sense of security, it is enough to take it by its collar or leash when climbing stairs. In order to take away the dog's fear of them, practice climbing stairs with it in a relaxed way. Use another dog that happily and confidently climbs stairs as a model. Also, introducing the command "slowly" to your dog can be helpful. This will prevent the dog from running too quickly on the stairs in its excitement and then tripping. If climbing stairs is unavoidable in your home, try to make it as pleasant an experience for your dog as possible. Make sure the stairway is well lit so that your dog can see the individual steps. Use carpet-tiles of different colors on the stairs. These are easily recognized by the dog—and then there will be no smooth steps to slip on!

Supportive help Dogs with joint or back problems should climb very few stairs. Ideally, they should not climb any at all.

Stairs and health

In principle, dogs with relatively long spines or a genetic tendency to joint and spine disease should climb as few stairs as possible. This also will help prevent these illnesses from occurring or slow down their progress, especially in elderly dogs. Although senior dogs can usually climb up stairs without too much difficulty, the way down is harder; their joints and spine are stressed by the brief stops they make on each step. This is why you should keep the number of stairs your dog climbs to a minimum when its build indicates this is called for or when there is an existing illness.

As seldom as possible

Using commands, you can limit your dog's sphere of activity to the ground floor (see p95) so that it does not follow you when you go down into the basement or upstairs. A dog does not necessarily have to have access to all the rooms in a dwelling; some areas can be off-limits. When dogs are suffering from dementia, or their vision is poor, block off the stairs with a baby gate to ensure that they cannot go up or down the stairs and fall in an unsupervised moment (see p147).

Hands-on help

One can carry smaller dogs up and down the stairs without too much difficulty. But when a dog has reached the substantial weight of 66 to 88 pounds (30–40 kilos), or even heavier, it is no longer always feasible to carry a dog without assistance. Perhaps you are fortunate and there is an elevator in your building that comfortably whisks you and your four-legged friend upstairs. Fortunately, an elevator is fairly common today in apartment buildings and public buildings. Practice taking elevators with your dog early on so that it is not afraid. If there is no elevator, and you live above the ground floor level, you will definitely have a problem if you have a heavy dog that cannot climb stairs. Not all dog owners are able or willing to move because of their dog. If you are fortunate, there always will be enough family members around to help carry the dog with unified strength when needed. If this is not the case, visit your neighbors and find out whose friendly help you can count when you need it. When no one is around who is willing to help, engage a dog sitter to come by on a regular schedule to help you carry your dog up and down the stairs. For all these reasons, it is important to think critically and objectively about your living circumstances when you decide to get a dog, especially if you plan on adopting an elderly dog.

Q WHY DOES MY DOG REFUSE TO CLIMB UP AN OPEN STAIRCASE?

A This is a common problem. Some dogs refuse to climb stairs because their legs once slipped between the individual treads. This either caused them pain, or at the very least shocked them. Other dogs are irritated simply by how an open staircase looks to them. This is understandable when you look at staircases from a dog's perspective: when climbing up a set of stairs, a dog looks directly into the gaps between the steps.

Practice taking elevators with your dog so that as it gets older it will be seen as a completely normal event.

A DOG TALE

Our eight-year-old Collie/German Shepherd mix Lucky decided at some point that the back of our minivan was his favorite place. He takes every opportunity of springing up into it. When a thunderstorm is brewing, he frantically insists on getting into the vehicle. We always knew that Lucky was a clever dog, but since he also seems to be well versed in the natural sciences, we've given him a perfect nickname—"The Physicist."

COLLAR OR HARNESS?

As a rule, a collar is usually a good choice for older dogs, too. Make sure that it is soft, not too tight, and fits properly. Avoid choke-chains or collars without stop-rings. Padded collars are available for shorthaired dogs and dogs with sensitive skin. It is usually a question of personal preference whether you opt for a collar or harness. However, a harness is the better choice for dogs suffering from spinal problems or those are that sensitive in the larynx area. A harness also lets you react quickly if you need to come to the aid of your dog. This can prove very helpful when your dog is old and not all that sure-footed. When choosing a harness, make sure that it fits perfectly and is well padded.

CAR

A dog that has become used to traveling with you in cars over the years does not usually, as a rule, have any problems with car travel when it is old. If you have adopted a dog when it is already elderly, test how it reacts when it is driven around in a car. If the dog is restless during a drive it might be feeling nauseous. Do not feed a dog just before a drive and make sure to stop often enough for breaks on longer drives. If your dog vomits or salivates heavily in the car, let your veterinarian know. Your dog can be prescribed a medication against motion sickness if necessary.

Safe traveling

As with every other type of cargo, dogs have to be safely secured in a vehicle and not be able to move freely about. Never let them sit on your lap or the passenger seat! Smaller dogs are best transported in special dog carriers. These should be placed at right angles to the direction of travel, either on the back seat or in a station wagon's luggage area, and securely fastened in place. If you have a large dog, a station wagon is especially practical; the dog can be transported in the luggage area behind a strong wire screen.

Getting in and out

We know many dogs that, even in advanced age, are able to hop up into cars with great agility. Other dogs find this much harder to do. Smaller, lighter, dogs are, of course, quickly lifted up into cars. However, not every dog owner is able to lift a heavy dog in and out of a car several times a day. To help out, quite a few dog owners have trained their pets to place their front legs on the tailgate. Then all that is needed is a little bit of a push on their behinds. An old blanket draped over the tailgate will help prevent scratches to the paint job or bumper. Pet stores also sell practical folding ramps that enable dogs to walk up easily into cars with a bit of training. Weekend carpenters can also build these portable ramps quite cheaply themselves.

If you own a heavy dog and are buying a new station wagon, it pays to take a close look at the loading area before purchasing it. The lower the tailgate, the easier it will be for your dog to jump into the vehicle.

GARDEN

Owning a garden is not an absolute must for dog owners! If a dog is given ample exercise and a variety of things to do, an apartment can also be perfectly adequate. A garden offers many advantages, especially for older dogs that have to relieve themselves at short intervals. Being able to let your dog go outside now and then without fuss often makes your day run more smoothly. Having a garden does not, however, free you from taking your dog out for regular walks. If there is a green space close to your apartment, such as a strip of grass that provides a place for your dog to relieve itself, then this is just as convenient as a garden. Just make sure you always have a plastic bag on hand to pick up any dog excrement.

With the right encouragement, and enough training, a dog can come to enjoy using a ramp.

Cold does not discomfort this dog, whose heavy coat keeps it warm. But dogs with thin coats can freeze easily in winter, or when it is wet outside.

WEATHER

How a very old or chronically ill dog feels can depend, among other things, on the weather. For example, it may feel tired when it is hot outside. Some dogs also feel weather changes. When it is cold and damp outside, its aged bones bother it, and, if cardiovascular illnesses have also been diagnosed, symptoms such as vomiting and panting can appear. If the dog's condition is fairly stable, these symptoms should fade away after one or two days. Still, do not blame all your senior dog's ailments on the weather—when in doubt, go and see your veterinarian.

IS LEAVING THE DOG AT HOME BEST?

If you are planning an excursion that might tire out your dog a great deal physically or mentally, then you should decide well in advance whether or not the dog really has to accompany you.

You will certainly have to plan any joint expeditions you decide to make with your senior dog's needs in mind. If, for example, your dog chills easily, and you plan on taking it into a restaurant that has a cold stone floor, take a blanket with you for the dog to lie on so that it does not catch a cold. Sometimes, though, it is better for all concerned for the dog to stay at home. In such cases, the best course of action is to arrange for someone to take care of your dog in its accustomed environment when you are away. For example, family members or other people your dog trusts can come into your home to care for it (*see p26*).

Holiday time is the best time of the year for both owner and dog—when the preparation is right!

VACATIONS

Each year, we humans look forward to vacation time. For a senior dog too, this can be the best time of the year since it has its owner to itself more often than usual. Our four-legged friend senses the relaxed holiday atmosphere and enjoys the shared time together.

Being well prepared

Travel with older dogs has to be carefully planned. If you plan on traveling to a foreign country, inquire at least four months ahead about current entry requirements. Some countries will quarantine pets, others require certificates of health provided by accredited veterinarians. If you are stopping off in a foreign country along the way, also check the rules applying to that country in relation to your final destination to avoid any unpleasant surprises. For travel within the US and Canada, find out what the regulations are for each state or province you intend to travel in. And finding out before you leave where and when your dog can run free in your vacation town, for example, will save precious holiday time.

Before leaving home, make a tag for your dog that lists both your home and vacation addresses and telephone numbers. Your dog will be returned to you more quickly if it wanders off. Also discuss with your veterinarian any special health risks that might be encountered at your destination and find out if there are any preventive medications your dog could take.

MODE OF TRAVEL

Even for young dogs, airplane or rail travel is very tiring. Traveling by car is easiest on everyone. A long car trip, especially in an air-conditioned vehicle, is usually not a problem for older dogs (see p42–3). Stop regularly so that your dog can relieve itself and have a drink of water. If you park your car in the sun or it is hot, never leave your dog in the car. A dog dehydrates very quickly.

Holiday homes or apartments are ideal for a vacation with the whole family, dog and all. These are more spacious than hotel rooms and you can arrange your daily routine to suit yourself. Also, not many hotels allow you to bring your dog into the dining room and therefore it will have to stay alone in your room at mealtimes.

PACKING YOUR SENIOR DOG'S SUITCASE

→ The appropriate health and veterinary certificates

→ Any relevant documents such as papers showing that your dog is a working dog (i.e. member of an international dog search team)

→ Its regular food (see p101–07)

→ Leash and collar

→ Tow line if needed (see p35)

→ Muzzle (depending on local regulations)

→ Food and water dishes

→ Toys

→ Treats and chew toys

→ Dog grooming kit

→ Suntan lotion (see p114)

→ Tick tweezers

→ Bed and blanket

→ Drying towel

→ Old sheets for covering up upholstered furniture

→ Dog shampoo

→ Dog first-aid kit (see p132) and any medicines your dog needs to take regularly

Have everything?
Pack your dog's suitcase very carefully.

Q **DO DOG KENNELS ALSO BOARD ELDERLY DOGS?**

A If your senior dog is still active and in good physical shape, you can also board it in a good kennel once you have reached your holiday destination. Perhaps your dog has already spent its holidays there and you have been very satisfied with the way your dog was treated. However, if this is the first time around, you should carefully check out the dog's lodgings. If possible, talk to other dog owners that have boarded their four-legged companions there. You should not experiment with older dogs. If your dog is aged, kenneling it is not an ideal solution since it will not always handle such a radical change to its routine very well.

CHECKING THINGS OUT

During the first few days of vacation you should take things easy. You and your senior dog need time to explore your new surroundings and adjust to the change in routine. Find out right away, just in case, where the nearest veterinarian or animal clinic is located. Should a visit to the veterinarian prove necessary and speed is crucial, you will be well prepared and not lose any valuable time getting help. Also, when choosing the country you are traveling to, remember that language differences might exist that could make it more difficult to describe your dog's condition to the veterinarian.

GOOD BEHAVIOR

Take care that your dog does not dirty carpets, upholstery or bedding. If your dog has to relieve itself frequently, you will have to take it outside for a short walk as often as is called for. However, if your dog is incontinent, it might be best to leave it at home in the first place. To avoid accidents, and if does not soil itself too often, your dog can lie on a rubber mat. In any case, your dog should rest and sleep in its dog bed and not be allowed to stretch out on the hotel bed or sofa. Should your dog damage or dirty the furniture, it goes without saying that you should report it and pay for the damage. Of course dogs may also bark in hotels now and then, but constant barking or howling greatly disturbs the other guests and taxes everyone's nerves. Always keep in mind that it is how you and all other dog owners behave that determines whether or not pets are welcome guests in holiday accommodations.

Be considerate of other guests. Make sure, for example, that your dog does not bark continuously.

IS YOUR DOG BETTER OFF AT HOME?

If your dog is already very old and suffers from health problems, you should think seriously about the wisdom of subjecting it to a vacation. A long car ride, especially if there are long traffic jams, and then completely new surroundings at the holiday destination, can lead to several very restless and tiring initial vacation days. Caring for a stressed dog, one that perhaps reacts to the changed environment with diarrhea and restlessness at night, entailing a visit to a strange veterinarian, is anything but relaxing for all concerned. In such cases, it is more sensible either not to travel at all or to travel without your dog.

OLD DOGS ARE LOVABLE
and sometimes expensive

Some older and elderly dogs are extremely healthy. But, depending on the kind of illness a dog has, treatment costs can add up to a sum that would usually be enough to finance the annual vacation—as we know too well.

Despite all your affection for your senior dog, do not forget that costs can be incurred for unscheduled visits to veterinarians and for therapy and treatments carried out by animal naturopaths and physical therapists. These are always extra costs, above and beyond the amount you would normally spend for vaccinations and other preventive treatments.

PREPARING AHEAD

When your financial situation is sound, it is advisable to set aside a nest egg for emergencies. If you own several dogs, the size of the nest egg should reflect their number. Many dog owners set up dedicated savings accounts into which they pay a set amount of money monthly.

There are also insurance policies just for dogs, although most insurance companies will only insure a dog if it is eight years old or younger. Sometimes, depending on a dog's breed or health history, a policy will exclude certain types of treatments. Policies range from those offering complete coverage, including vaccinations and other preventive treatments, to partial coverage just for surgery and postoperative care. Sometimes there is a yearly reimbursement cap, or a cap at double the veterinarian's fees. Have your veterinarian advise you about types of coverage and contract terms to ensure that the policy you are thinking about purchasing offers the kind of protection that you you may need.

WHEN A SENIOR DOG MOVES IN

MANY PEOPLE AUTOMATICALLY think about getting a puppy when they have decided to expand their family to include a dog. It means a great deal to them to be able to accompany the puppy as it grows up—and to be there as it first cautiously and clumsily explores the big wide world. Why, then, should you choose to take in an old dog at all if you can purchase or adopt a puppy? Many dog owners that have taken in a four-legged senior have certainly had this question put to them by family and friends—and more than once. After all, the probability that the dog will become sick as it ages is high and so the time remaining to spend together will most likely be less than when a young four-legged dog becomes part of your family.

There are, however, many reasons for choosing a dog that is more or less elderly. Some people lack the time to care properly for a puppy and train it. Others appreciate the calmness and even-temperedness of an older dog. Perhaps, when they visited an animal shelter to choose an animal, their hearts were utterly won over by a senior canine even though they had initially decided to adopt a younger one. Whatever the reasons for adopting an old dog, we do not know anyone who has regretted making this decision—throughout times both good and bad.

CAREFUL PLANNING

He knows what he wants
Older dogs often demonstrate a
decided personality.

Many dog owners are fans of gray-muzzled dogs. They
treasure their even-temperedness and the great
life experience revealed in their soft eyes, experience
a younger dog first has to gain.

Some people deliberately want to adopt a dog that has lost its home. They
want to give it a second chance at having a secure place to stay and being
part of a family until its final days.

When chance does not bring you, the future owner of a senior dog, and a
four-legged friend together, you should think carefully—before the dog moves
in—about the breed or type of dog which will best suit your personality and
best fit into your lifestyle. Sketching this out on paper might come in handy
when you have narrowed down the choice to a dog that does not conform
to the idea you originally had. You can then better judge whether or not the
compromises called for will prevent you from taking in this dog.

A DOG TALE

Nine years ago, we adopted Nicky,
a seven-year-old Afghan Hound.
Everyone expressed doubts given his
advanced age. But Nicky was the
perfect dog for us, even though he had
many idiosyncrasies that had already
given him the reputation of being a
difficult dog. We took these into
account and never experienced any
problems. He lived to be 13 years old.
He enriched our lives and influenced
them enormously. There were ups and
downs of course, but we would do it
again at the drop of a hat.

LARGE OR SMALL?

A dog's size and weight affect not only its life expectancy (*see p14*), but
also many areas of your daily life (*see p38–44*). For instance, what about
the size of your car? Does the car you now own offer a large dog enough
space—especially if it travels with a great deal of luggage? Another
important consideration is whether or not you are able to properly control
a large dog when it is on the leash. Even an impeccably well-behaved dog
can, in an unexpected moment, lunge forward with all its might.

A large dog and a small
car—this will not do! On the
road a dog has to be
securely stowed away.
Sitting on the passenger
seat is absolutely taboo!

Two terriers:
A purebred West Highland White Terrier and a Jack Russell-mix—both utterly lovable terriers!

Then you will have to summon up a lot of strength to be able to pull back the dog successfully. Would-be dog owners who are small in stature or unsure how physically fit they are should probably opt for a medium or small-sized senior canine companion, one they can control.

PUREBRED OR MIXED-BREED?

Individual preferences often determine what kind of purebred or mixed-breed dog a person decides to get. Some people are fond of one breed of dog and no other type will ever come into question. If one or more dogs of this breed once lived in your family, you can usually better predict the dog's needs and know whether or not you are up to the challenges it will entail. If this is your first dog, and you would like a purebred, a wealth of detailed information about the breed's characteristics is available. Sources include other dog owners, breeders, animal shelter workers and animal rescue groups dedicated to this breed, veterinarians, and dog trainers. Important points to ask about are, for example, temperament, how much the dog needs to be kept busy, and how much exercise it needs. Find out what the original occupation of the dog's ancestors was. Also ask whether or not the dog is usually easy to train or whether you will need to use your imagination and exercise a great deal of patience.

"Some people are fond of one breed of dog..."

Every mixed-breed dog is unique,
but the owners of purebred dogs say the same thing about their dogs.

Q **ARE OLDER DOGS SUIT-
ABLE FOR BEGINNERS?**

A Senior dogs often make good
dogs for first-time dog owners.
Their temperament and
nature is known. They are
usually socially competent
and they already have been
trained. Animal shelters
harbor many uncomplicated
canines that can help new
dog owners gather learning
experience while giving them
much pleasure. Of course,
some elderly dogs have
behavioral problems (*see
p65*) and do not lend
themselves to being cared for
by first-time owners. Such
dogs need to be cared for
by experienced people who
knowingly take on all the
challenges they pose and
deal competently with them.

It is much more difficult to evaluate mixed-breed dogs. Their ancestry is
not always known or cannot be readily determined just by looking at the
dog, and one never knows what genetic tendencies are dominant in a mixed
breed, both good and bad.

Every dog is unique

Even purebred dogs that look absolutely identical to each other on the outside
differ greatly in nature to one another. No one dog is like another. Along
with its genetic makeup, the experiences a dog has had in life and its
previous training determine to a great extent how a dog's personality and
behavior developed over the course of time. These factors play a significant
role, especially when a dog is older. After all, the dog had at least one owner
before you, or perhaps has made even more stops in its life. Everything has
contrived to make the dog into what it is today. For this reason, it is best to
throw all great expectations overboard and judge the candidates, with all
their strengths and weakness, without prejudice.

AGE AND HEALTH

Certainly, when choosing a new dog, you should not leave age and health
out of the equation. Old does not always mean the same thing. Both
physically and psychologically, huge differences exist between dogs of the
same age (*see p13*). Many kind individuals deliberately and knowingly
choose to adopt a senior dog that requires a great deal of care because they
want to ensure that its life has a happy ending.
Others have decided to take in a senior dog but set
great store on its being in good health. They would
like to undertake many activities with the dog, or,
at the least, share many years of life with it. Before
making a final decision, you must decide for
yourself how much you are prepared to give, and
how much you can give.

At seventeen, this female Dachshund
is dependent on the helping hands of
her owner so that she can move about
outside without faltering.

THE LITTLE DIFFERENCE

A dog's sex does not usually play a significant role in the choice of a senior dog. Many future dog owners have already had good experience with a dog or a bitch and, for this reason, would like their new four-legged friend to be of the same sex. Also, many elderly dogs have been already neutered and therefore puppies are not an issue.

If a dog has been neutered, it is of no significance whether they are young or old. The reasons a dog owner decides for or against a specific sex are the same. For example, there is no menopause in dogs and bitches go into heat about twice a year. Male dogs of all ages mark their territory frequently during walks and can be aggressive toward other male dogs. Our experience has shown that its sex does not make a dog more affectionate or easier to control. Especially in the case of a senior dog, it comes down much more to the dog's nature, its training, and its past experiences as well as the dog owner's personality and how consistent she or he is.

If, however, a dog already lives in your home, the choice of a male or female dog can be very important to the harmonious coexistence of the two dogs (see p67).

A dog's sex is irrelevant when it comes to aging. This ten-year-old bitch looks old but she is still very fit.

FINANCIAL CONSIDERATIONS

Many elderly dogs are sound and healthy. However, if you adopt one, there is a high probability that, within a short time, you will incur veterinary costs that exceed what you would normally pay for a young dog (see p47).

There are always sick dogs at animal shelters waiting for new homes. Luckily, there are also many foster parents who take in such dogs. Sometimes they pay the veterinarian's fees themselves, but often a shelter will pay the fees or have the shelter's veterinarian treat the dog. This ensures that finding a good home for a dog with dog-lovers will not fail due to lack of funds.

Still, cost factors should never play a central role in the decision for or against an older dog. When you take home a puppy, you also know that the dog will become ill at some point. Whoever takes in a dog, regardless of its age, must always be able to provide the best possible care for their dog.

This ten-year-old male dog looks fairly youthful but he is already suffering from serious physical ailments.

Faithful soul
The liveliness, devotion, and nature of a dog depend on several things. A dog's sex is just one factor among many.

Dominant leaders give their dogs security and firm direction, and can control them with very few words.

WHAT CAN I OFFER?

When you decide to bring a dog into your home you are taking on a great responsibility. If the dog is already old, this responsibility will probably not last for too many years but at the same time will be a harder one for you to bear. You will have to consider seriously whether or not you are capable of offering a canine companion—whatever its age—everything it needs. Living together with another individual—whether human or dog—always entails making compromises. When these are not seen as giving up something but are made freely, both parties will be happy and their lives enriched. A dog will be happy when it is provided with a stable environment that is tailored to its needs. You should also assume the role of dominant pack leader to your dog (*see p86–87*), and offer it consistency, adequate physical exercise, and plenty of activities as well as appropriate food, grooming, and medical care.

Of course, every member of the family and, if required, the landlord, have to agree to your taking in a dog. If you do not do this, another home might have to be found for the dog and then tears will flow.

Consider the following possible scenarios:

Depending on its past experiences, the dog refuses to remain at home alone. Either it has not learned how to do so, or it suffers from separation anxiety (*see p55*). Sometimes this problem can be mitigated or corrected. Unfortunately, some dogs absolutely cannot tolerate being separated from their owners. If this is the case, either a member of your family will always have to stay at home with the dog, or you will always have to take it with you. This calls for good organization.

A large property is ideal for dogs but, if they are given plenty of activity, not essential.

The dog might require intensive care if it becomes ill. Is there always someone at home (*see p26*)?

If you are unsure about taking in a dog for the rest of its life, and offering it a home that gives it safety and security, it is better to abandon the idea altogether. Perhaps a canine companion will better fit into your life a few years down the road. The worst situation that can arise, and should be avoided, is when a dog is turned into a kind of wandering trophy and constantly transferred from owner to owner.

Senior meets senior

Many seniors choose deliberately to take in an aged dog. Either they cannot cope with the work involved in properly training a puppy, or they are afraid that a young dog will outlive them. This is an ideal combination of two- and four-legged seniors. Often, retired people are in search of something to occupy themselves and they have extra time on their hands to devote to a dog. For instance, a dog that has an illness and needs more care is in good hands here.

But it is also important that seniors choose dogs that do not overtax their own physical limits due to

Caring for a dog gives older people an occupation. In return, they receive affection and devotion.

their strength or the amount of activity they require. Even if you have had large dogs in your family for the past thirty years it is better to go down a notch when you are sixty or seventy years of age. Dogs that are ten or eleven years old—and older—often can demonstrate surprising, and sudden, strength that needs to be controlled and funneled into the proper channels. Always think about what might happen when your dog tugs on its leash or springs up at you. When you are old, your balance and stability might not be quite as good as they once were, and falls can have very serious consequences.

No matter whether they are young or old, every dog owner should write down who they would like to have take care of their dog when they can no longer do so. Best is having the dog live with a person it already trusts.

Q WHAT IS SEPARATION ANXIETY?

A The diagnosis "separation anxiety" is often made when a dog barks, howls, or ransacks the house when its owners are away. However, very few dogs suffer from real separation anxiety. Instead, they are letting their frustration out at having to stay at home alone. Training can help control this kind of behavior. Real separation anxiety shows itself through behavior a dog cannot control such as excessive salivation or shaking. The cause is often the loss once— or even more—of someone it loved. Or the cause might be poor training in the past. Chances are slim that one day a dog suffering from separation anxiety will be able to stay calmly at home alone. Still, you should try to manage this type of anxiety since reducing its severity helps both animal and human.

"When you decide to bring a dog into your home, you are taking on a great responsibility."

Many animal rescue groups specialize in finding new homes for purebred dogs.

CHOOSING A SENIOR DOG

There are many reasons why senior dogs lose their homes. Many end up in animal shelters because their owners have moved, divorced, or have no time to spare.

Others are surrendered to a shelter because their previous owners could no longer care for them due to illness or death. Unfortunately too, many wonderful dogs are evicted from their homes simply because their owners considered them too much of a bother.

Once you have thought about all the pros and cons of giving a senior dog a home, and are certain you can provide it with the best possible environment, then it is time to begin the search for a new housemate.

WHERE TO FIND SENIOR DOGS

The first step is to discover where the nearest animal shelter is located and pay it a visit. Very often, many lovable senior dogs are waiting there for a new family to adopt them. If you have decided you would like a purebred dog, the best place to turn to is an animal rescue group that specializes in finding homes for dogs of a specific breed such as Grayhounds or Golden Retrievers. But you might also find the dog of your dreams through studying newspaper ads, watching animal adoption programs on television, or researching on the Internet. Sometimes, too, dog breeders will give away dogs that they no longer want to use for breeding. As critical as one can be about this practice, it is often the best outcome for the dog.

LISTEN TO YOUR HEART

It quite often happens that people wanting to adopt a dog fall in love with one bearing absolutely no resemblance to the dog they had initially imagined. The male dog they wanted ends up being a female, the elegant purebred a loyal mixed-breed dog. Instead of an energetic pint-sized dog, a 66-pound (30kg) "lap-dog" stretches out full-length on the couch. Often, it is just a matter of chemistry: when you look into a dog's eyes, or when a dog does not once leave your side, something simply clicks between dog and human. Although being objective is important when you are choosing a dog, you should still listen to your feelings and trust your intuition. Of course, you have to be able to offer the dog the kind of home it needs. A Siberian Husky, for example, would not be very happy in a bachelor apartment in the city. Even if you do so with a heavy heart, you will be showing a great deal of responsibility when you decide not to adopt a dog that is unsuited to your lifestyle.

Trust your feelings, and keep your criteria in mind, then you will most certainly find a dog that suits you perfectly.

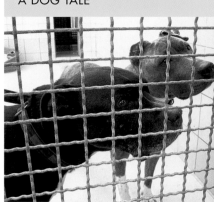

A DOG TALE

This past summer, due to a lifestyle change, I was finally able to realize my dream of owning a dog. I went to the animal shelter to look at one Staffordshire Terrier—and fell in love with two—Daisy and Tony, each eleven years old. Since Tony had been living in the shelter for seven years, we thought long and hard about it. Could he ever get used to a new environment and should we risk it? We visited the dogs often, had many talks with the shelter's workers, and decided, finally, to take home both dogs. From the very first day, they made themselves right at home and it seemed as though they had always lived with us. Even after several years in a shelter, dogs are capable of adjusting to new homes.

COLLECTING INFORMATION

Give yourself plenty of time when you are choosing your future canine housemate. For example, take the dog you think you would like out on long walks with the entire family. Find out as much as you possibly can about its

past experiences by asking the former owner or animal shelter's workers about them. The more you know about a dog's previous life, the better you can judge whether or not it will suit you. Take some time to think about questions important to you and write them down in a list (*see below*).

Sometimes, however, there is no information, or very little, to be had about an animal's previous life. If this is the case, you will have to try to size up the dog as best as you can during your initial meetings. If you are still unsure, then a good dog trainer can give you helpful advice.

When a dog's past is completely unknown
you will need to discover what the dog knows and does not know. Cautiously approach daily objects and common situations with your new friend.

IMPORTANT QUESTIONS TO ASK WHEN YOU ARE CHOOSING A SENIOR DOG

' How does the dog behave toward children?

' Does it show any reservations toward certain people? If so, then toward whom? What kind of behavior does it show?

' Does it get along well with other dogs or, for example, does one have to watch out when encountering other dogs of a certain breed or sex?

' Is the dog used to being driven in vehicles?

' Can it stay at home alone?

' Is the dog allowed to run free and does it return when called?

' Can the dog follow any commands? If so, which ones?

' Does the dog need regular medication or some sort of special veterinary care? If so, then how much money should one plan on spending?

' How is the dog's health? Has it had any previous illnesses, or sustained injuries? Does it have any disabilities? If so, then how do they affect its daily life? Is it possible that they will lead to further complaints with advanced age?

' Are there any other things I need to take into account in order to care properly for the dog?

SETTLING IN

Before your new housemate moves in with you, you should have all its food and equipment ready.

This also means, if possible, providing the kind of food the dog has been accustomed to. If you want to feed the dog a different kind of food, then wait until it has adjusted to its new environment (*see p103*).

How quickly an older dog comes to trust its new environment and its new people depends on a good many factors. Some canine companions will step right over the doorstep into their new home, sniff everything that can be sniffed, devour the food set out for them with great appetite, and then go to lie in their baskets—they have arrived home! Others need somewhat longer and might seek out a corner from which to observe—from a safe distance—the household comings and goings. This can last for days or even weeks. Yet, at some point, a wet nose will push against your hand—a silent signal that it is high time for a pat.

Allowing a dog to take all the time that it needs to make contact with you on its own terms is the best approach. Still, shy dogs might have to be bribed with treats to encourage them to overcome their shyness. Other dogs will thaw when you play around in front of them with an interesting toy. However, if a dog is very fearful, then it is a good idea to seek the advice of a dog trainer. Together you will come up with a clever strategy for conquering the animal's heart.

NEW BEGINNINGS

Three things are very important: patience, understanding, and clear rules (*see p86–92*). Always remember that adjusting to a new environment and new people is both a huge challenge and a huge chance for the dog—and many dogs adapt much more readily than expected. It is up to you to try to make up for, as much as you can, the mistakes and negligence of the past.

"Give yourself plenty of time when you are choosing your future canine housemate."

On the bright side
Being given a new home gives many dogs an opportunity to lead a regulated life with dedicated people.

The way an older dog relates to children depends largely on the kinds of experiences it has had with them in the past.

CHECKING OUT YOUR NEW COMPANION

In the first few weeks after you have brought home a senior dog, have the veterinarian give it a thorough checkup. Knowing exactly what state of health your dog is in will give you certainty. And, should an illness be diagnosed, you will be able to take steps early on. If the dog is healthy, then you will have valuable points of comparison for later examinations on hand. If your dog is fearful, wait until it has come to trust you and feels safe in its new environment before taking it to be examined.

The next step is to find out how well the dog is coping with, and adapting to, its new home and lifestyle. Perhaps the dog's previous owner or the animal shelter's workers have passed on a few good tips about its behavior. Even so, sometimes a dog will react quite differently than expected in a new home—and sometimes better than expected—so it certainly pays to test out its reactions yourself.

Behavior toward people

Observe your senior dog as it interacts with many different kinds of people. How does it behave, for example, toward children, men, women, people using a cane, holding a baseball bat, or wearing a hat, bicyclists, joggers, or in-line skaters? Since you never can know what kinds of negative experiences a senior dog has had in the past or what parts of its training were neglected, it might react unexpectedly with people. You do not have to test out everything in the course of a few days. Find out about these things when the opportunity arises. Otherwise you will place both yourself and your dog under unnecessary stress.

Behavior toward dogs and other animals

The way a dog reacts to other dogs also affects daily life (see p33–37). Is the senior dog socially competent and uncomplicated with other dogs? Some dogs are, for example, very easy-going outside their homes, but they do not brook the presence of any other dogs in their houses or gardens since they have very strong territorial instincts. Check out how it behaves toward other animals as well (see p36–37).

"This is my home here!"
On their own territory, dogs can demonstrate completely different behavior than they do during a walk.

Talk to other dog owners to ensure that your new dog has contact, at first, only with easy-going dogs.

Housebreaking a dog

Dogs are very clean animals and they usually do not soil their own living quarters. Surprisingly, even older dogs that previously were kept in cages are often housebroken. As soon as you bring your new dog home, take it to the place outside where you want it to relieve itself in future. It will certainly remember this spot.

Unfortunately, some dogs, such as rescued dogs, will have endured terrible conditions under their previous owners and have either never been housebroken at all or have forgotten their training.

Take your new dog out for a walk as often as possible. When it has become acclimatized, you can reduce the number of times you take it out.

You will have to start housebreaking such dogs in much the same way as you would train a puppy. Take it outside every two hours. Also take it outside after it has woken up, eaten, played, or shown signs of restlessness, and when it is excited. Always go to the same place. When exiting the house, use the door you use when you are going on a walk with your dog so that it makes the right connections immediately. The following are signs that a dog has to relieve itself: restlessness, running in a circle, staring at you, turning around, sniffing the floor, going to the door, and whining or barking.

Praise your dog when it relieves itself at the place you have selected. Reward it with delicious treats. Pick and use a specific command to encourage your dog such as "it's time now" or "do it." Later on, many dogs are prompted to relieve themselves when they hear these words.

If you allow your dog to sleep in your bedroom at night (see p86), you will certainly notice its restlessness if it urgently needs to relieve itself and will be able to take it outside quickly. Otherwise, you should limit the dog's sphere of movement to the room where, in future, it will spend its nights. It would be ideal if you, too, spent the first few nights in this room—on the sofa in the living room, for example. Allowing a new dog to have the run of the house at night is inadvisable. The dog might well wander around the house in search of a remote corner to relieve itself in so as not to soil its nest. And, when you are choosing a room for your dog to sleep in, remember that dogs are often attracted to carpets when they need to relieve themselves because the urine is readily absorbed.

If, despite all your precautions, the dog leaves a little souvenir in the house you must not tell it off or rub its nose into the mess. It will not able to associate one act with the other. On no account should you hit your dog! If you catch your dog in the act, show your displeasure by shaking your head and grumbling. Take your dog to the place of elimination as quickly as you can. If you only later discover the accident, clean it up without the dog's seeing it and without comment. In future, pay more attention to the signals the dog sends. Once your new dog has become accustomed to your routine you will be able to reduce the number of walks it needs to relieve itself.

If the dog sleeps near you, you will certainly know when it needs to go outside to relieve itself.

Acoustic and visual irritants

After it has moved into a new environment, a dog is exposed to completely new sounds. Does it know what a vacuum cleaner sounds like, a television, a doorbell, an air-compressor, or shutters banging harmlessly in the wind? How will the dog react when it hears a loud bang, such as a thunderclap, a firecracker, or a backfiring motorcycle? Many dogs remain absolutely calm, others are spooked easily (see p65–66). Visual signals can also provoke very different reactions. Some senior dogs are always calm and collected, nothing fazes them; others begin trembling at the sight of such seemingly harmless things as banners or posters flapping in the wind or birthday balloons bobbing up and down over a table.

A DOG TALE

When my Ibizan Podenco bitch Lena arrived in my home the sound of the television set sent her into a complete panic. To get her used to it, I simply left the set on at a low volume for an hour every now and then. When Lena showed no reaction to the background noise, I raised the volume bit by bit until the sound of the television set was at a normal level. In just a few days Lena no longer feared the television set and in fact ignored it completely.

Their good hearing makes dogs very sensitive to sounds—even those humans cannot hear.

TRAINING YOUR NEW DOG

When people take a dog into their home that has had a previous owner, they often make the mistake of coddling it in order to try and make up for the dog's tragic past or its stay in an animal shelter. But this is, unquestionably, the wrong thing to do.

Perhaps the new dog already knows a few commands. This makes dealing with it on a daily basis, and its adjustment phase, much easier.

SYMPATHETIC BUT CONSISTENT

Make good use of this new start. By setting clear rules and boundaries, you will be giving your new elderly dog security! Be understanding, authoritative, and always consistent. If something is forbidden once, it should always be forbidden. From the first day onward, you are the one that sets the house rules, not the dog. Is the dog allowed on the sofa or not? Is the kitchen out-of-bounds or not? Discuss all the basic rules with your family so that they understand the reasons behind them and everyone follows them consistently. You will have a better chance of success if everyone enforces the rules in the same way. Each time an exception is made the dog will be irritated, and this will make its adjustment to its new home more difficult. And making exceptions sets precedents and your dog might well come to think the exception is the rule. It is very time-consuming to set the dog straight later on.

Professional help

If you do not have very much experience dealing with dogs or are uncertain about how to deal with your new dog, then enlist the help of a good dog trainer. Having a trainer at your side from the very beginning ensures that no mistakes will creep in that will need undoing later on. Also, many dog trainers can be retained throughout the process of choosing your dog. They will help you pick the dog that is just right for you. This can be especially helpful when you already have one dog and you are adding another (*see p67*). But, should problems crop up later on, get some professional advice.

If a dog knows nothing about obedience, then you will have to begin with basic training and teach it the most important commands.

NOT FOR BEGINNERS

All those who let themselves in for a dog adventure for the first time are best advised to choose an uncomplicated dog. Of course, an older dog always brings some old baggage along with it. However, when its past crops up in the form of behavioral problems, experience is needed in order to do justice to both dog and human. Even if one has a great deal of enthusiasm to offer, a beginner would be overwhelmed!

We do not intend to deal in depth here with behavioral problems because this topic alone can fill a book. However, we think it is important to discuss two things that often cause daily problems since the affected dog is, at least at the beginning, difficult to control.

The strong dog

Strength here does not refer only to a dog's physical strength, but more importantly to its mental strength. Dogs like these will come up with many ways of strengthening their position in the family. For example, they will defend their sleeping spot, toy, or food by growling or snapping, or they want to be the one that chooses the direction of the walk or they bite the leash. Others refuse to be left alone; behave aggressively toward other dogs, even female dogs; prevent visitors from entering the home; or even try to attack them. Many do not respond to their owners when let off the leash outside, behaving as though they are independent. If these dogs do not have an experienced and authoritative handler, they can demonstrate problematic, sometimes dangerous, behavior.

The fearful dog

Fearful dogs, and dogs that panic easily, are also often difficult to control. When they are alarmed, they will not listen when you try to talk to them. They show flight response and can behave defensively if they feel threatened.

Never attempt to comfort a dog that is demonstrating fearful behavior with loving and well-meaning words. Giving it your attention and affection at this time will signal the dog that there is something to be afraid of—its fear is justified. This will only make things worse. To make your dog feel secure, the best reaction on your part is to remain utterly unimpressed by its behavior.

Extremely aggressive behavior must be countered with a great deal of experience and knowledge of dogs, and channeled into the proper paths.

Avoids eye contact

Ears are flattened back

The fearful dog

Submissive body language

When a dog becomes panic-stricken in a given situation, ignore it completely. Not only would any attempt to reach it fail because it is under so much stress at this moment, but also any sort of reassurance you give to the dog would be confirmation that its behavior is justified.

If the dog still can be talked to, and reacts to your lead, you can send it positive signals by acting cheerfully, and, without praising it, leading it past the situation it felt threatened by. You can also deflect its attention by repeating a simple training exercise or playing with it.

You should never tell off a fearful dog, or force it to confront whatever scares it. To counteract the problem, work up a training plan with a good dog trainer that will, step by step, help the dog get used to the kind of situation that triggers its fear.

Deflect the dog's attention before its fear intensifies. Having it search for hidden treats is one way of doing this.

A SECOND DOG JOINS THE FAMILY

More and more dog owners would love to have another canine companion at their side and are thinking seriously about bringing a second one into their home.

Most dog's lives are enriched whey they live with another dog and there are very few dogs that are unable to live with another member of their species because they have been poorly socialized. But what kind of canine partner will best suit your current dog?

GETTING THE RIGHT MIX

An important factor is how the dogs will get along together. Two confident and dominant dogs of the same sex and pack status will not get along too well. This means there is a much higher probability that there will be some conflict. However, a more dominant dog will show great tolerance toward a dog that is immediately submissive toward it. The better the dogs get along, the more harmonious living together will be.

Even dogs of the same sex can get along well once they sort out which one is dominant. If this is not settled, conflicts can arise. Serious fights certainly will occur if two dogs cannot tolerate each other at all. Then it will be almost impossible for the two dogs to dwell under the same roof. Since parting with the new dog might prove emotionally difficult, consider your decision well before bringing the second dog home.

A DOG TALE

When Angelo, our fourth dog, moved in with us, our two Podenco Canario bitches Jule and Nela were already eleven and eight years old respectively.

Both ignored the newcomer and demonstrated their unhappiness by pointedly looking away. When Angelo failed to maintain the proper distance, they snapped at him, but at least didn't use their teeth. It took a long time before the two elderly ladies became used to the changed situation and accepted Angelo. But our patience paid off; after a few months, they permitted Angelo to lie down with them and enjoy physical nearness.

A great team
When the combination is right, a dog can wish for nothing more than a canine companion at its side.

A heavy-weight and a bantam
Despite the size difference, these two dogs have great fun with each other and enjoy exciting adventures.

Size and breed

The size or breed of a dog does not determine what order in the hierarchy it will assume. There are many little dogs that, unchallenged, lord it over much larger dogs and play with them at length. Some large dominant dogs willingly lower themselves to the ground in order to play with small comrades on their own level.

It is possible that dogs of the same breed or type primarily will want to have more to do with each other than with other dogs since they usually have the same activity level and exercise needs. They also play in the same way. But there is no guarantee that once the dogs are brought together they will play happily together.

YOUR CURRENT DOG'S ROLE

No matter how old it is, if your current dog is experienced and sure of itself, it will often impart a sense of self-assuredness to a shy or insecure new dog. Your dog becomes a hero and role-model for the newcomer.
Many older dogs experience a second spring when a young dog moves in with them. They have to maintain their position and thus become more active and participate more in family life. Some, in fact, develop maternal or paternal feelings and help bring up the newcomer.

The first time at the ocean
The senior checks out the unfamiliar element, the junior waits in the background.

On the other hand, some dogs do not want to have anything at all to do with the new bundle of energy that has moved into their territory. After all, they not only create a disturbance but also mess up the well-established and cherished routine. Some dogs choose to beat a hasty retreat; others chastise the new dog more severely than is justified. There are also loner dogs that should not be brought together with a puppy since they might bite it badly. If you have the feeling that your senior dog will be overwhelmed by a puppy, opt for an older or, at least, calmer second dog.

In any case, your present dog should possess good obedience skills and its training should be reliable. It also should have passed through the early stages of development (*see p70*). It will be easier on your nerves if you can easily handle the dog you already have. Dealing with two energetic dogs, both of which have been badly brought up, at the same time can be very tiring. There are many possible dog pairings—the ideal one for you is best decided on a case-by-case basis.

Keeping its cool,
even when being pestered by a youngster, is not every old dog's strength. Some dogs will not tolerate pushy behavior from other dogs.

A DOG TALE

At nine years of age, our Afghan Hound Nicky had already become quite lazy; her favorite activity was sleeping on the sofa. Then, three-year-old Shalim stormed into our lives. From day one, Nicky was the boss. Although they never became best friends, and only played together extensively when they were outside, our senior dog blossomed after the arrival of the adolescent. Now she had a duty to perform—even if it was only putting Shalim in his proper place! Shalim profited from Nicky's self-assuredness and the example she set, something he really needed given his difficult past.

"It will be easier on your nerves if you can easily handle the dog you already have."

THINGS TO KEEP IN MIND

Double everything
Adding a second dog entails, of course, more costs than for one—such as for food, toys, and veterinary costs.

Two dogs afford their human a great deal of joy but they also usually mean more work and more expense than just one. Only add another set of paws to your dog-human pack if you are really sure you have the time to spend and can afford to keep a second one. Even though two dogs can amuse each other and provide each other with company, they still should not spend more time without your company than a single dog would. Along with the greater expense for equipment, food, veterinary costs, and dog grooming products, do not underestimate the time factor. You will have to double the time planned for combing, brushing, and other grooming. Training and showing affection will also require much more of your time since each dog needs individual attention. This will ensure that each dog follows orders unhesitatingly and the bond with you remains strong. And, if you have two dogs and one is older and one younger, for example, you will have to plan more daily walks and sometimes take the dogs on separate walks so that the senior is not overtaxed and the junior gets enough exercise.

If neither dog has been properly trained or they have problems relating to other dogs, walking them can be very stressful. They might pull on their leashes, or bare their teeth when they encounter other dogs, or not come when called.

If you own more than one dog, joint excursions will also be more difficult to plan. While you might be a welcome guest on vacation or at a friend's house with only one dog in tow, this might not be the case when you turn up with more than one. You will need to check this out beforehand. In fact, most excursions will have to be well organized ahead of time.

You also will need enough room in your house to place two dog beds properly (*see p38*) and to allow the dogs to stay out of each other's way when they are not getting along too well.

THINGS TO CONSIDER WHEN CHOOSING A SECOND DOG

KEY FACTORS	EXAMPLE
Adaptability and tolerance	If your current dog is very self-confident and determined, the newcomer will have to submit to it.
Care needed	Longhaired dogs need more grooming than shorthaired ones.
Size	Take into account the amount of space two dogs will require (house/car).
Exercise needed	A two-year-old dog will need much more exercise than a twelve-year-old dog.
Training	If your present dog does not obey consistently, then a second one should not move in.
Age	Your present dog already should have gone through the first stages of its development (1 to 1½ years, depending on the breed).

A dream team
The company of a younger female dog brings pep and zest into this senior dog's daily life.

WORK HARD—STAY YOUNG

AS THE YEARS GO BY, THE AMOUNT and type of activity a senior dog needs changes as it slows down. But, no matter what a dog's age, it is essential to the dog's health that both its physical and mental powers are exercised to their full capacity. Good ideas and some creativity are called for to prevent boredom from setting in or a dog's talents from being under-utilized.

Very often, elderly dogs are put out to pasture much too early, but both physical and mental activities can be tailored to your dog's state of health. Especially when a senior dog is already suffering from physical limitations, or is ill, it can be kept occupied—and its condition improved—through the challenge of mental exercise. Given their life experience, senior dogs are usually excellent problem-solvers and they are always interested in being given new challenges to tackle and overcome.

Even when you have reduced the length and speed of your daily walks together, give your routine variety by discovering new places and taking new paths. Along the way, have your dog practice some of the basic training commands or play games with it. When motivated enough, elderly dogs take great pleasure in experiencing and learning new things.

ACTIVITY IS A GOOD THING

Exercise is essential for elderly dogs. Daily outings strengthen their muscles, keep their joints supple, and strengthen their cardiopulmonary systems.

Regular physical activities that are tailored to your dog's needs will aid in maintaining its slim figure and level of fitness, and will strengthen its immune system. Provided they have good homes, good nutrition, proper grooming, and regular veterinary checkups, many senior dogs will remain physically active until late in life.

In good form
By exercising your dog regularly, you can do a great deal toward ensuring that it stays fit and enjoys physical activity for a long time.

Gray Power
Good musculature helps your dog move easily, supports its skeleton, and takes the strain off its joints.

FINDING THE RIGHT BALANCE

If you and your dog have been together for many years, you know very well how much activity it enjoys having. You also know exactly the kinds of physical activity your dog needs and which exercises tire it out happily but do not overtax its strength.

"You know the kinds of activity your dog needs."

When your dog begins exercising, make sure that it at first performs fluid movements, for example, by running on flat terrain rather than chasing a ball or another dog. This will give its muscles, sinews, and tendons a chance to warm up to operating temperature. Even athletes avoid cold starts in order to prevent injuring or overexerting themselves.

As your dog becomes older, there are fewer physical exercise routines that will suit it. Reduce or avoid all activities that will place stress on its joints and spine or could lead to pain or injury (see chart). If your canine companion is already suffering from deterioration of the joints due to a disease such as arthritis, it is probably best to avoid such activities altogether.

The amount of physical activity that elderly dogs need depends on how athletic they were in the past. Compared with other dogs of the same age, dogs who have had agility training, and other very athletic dogs that had regular training for years and perhaps even competed, are usually much more active when they become old. If you own a dog like this, it is very important to scale back its training regime slowly and systematically, just as with a human athlete. However, make sure to maintain some of that good physical condition when it is older.

THE RIGHT KIND OF ACTIVITY

VERY GOOD	TRY TO AVOID
Fluid movements	Wild jumping up and down
Trotting on level surfaces	Adventurous climbing
Soft, springy surfaces such as forest paths	Turning, abrupt stops and sprinting
Swimming	Extreme flexing of the spine (i.e. in obstacle courses)
Endurance training	Running long distances on hard surfaces

PREVENTING COLDS

Senior dogs that have sparse coats or suffer from chronic illnesses can easily get chilled in cold and damp weather (see p25). Small dogs, in particular, can get completely wet bellies simply by running through grass that is damp with morning dew. And, after walks in the rain, longhaired dogs often take hours to dry out properly. For this reason, keep a few old towels handy in your car and near the door of your house so that you can thoroughly rub down your dog after a walk. Not only will you help prevent your dog from getting a cold or another illness, you also will reduce the amount of dirt the dog tracks into your home.

DO NOT SPOIL YOUR DOG

Even when you are very concerned about your dog's condition, you should not pamper it. Make sure it performs a minimum amount of exercise—an amount set by you—each day. Some canines become quite lazy and complacent over the years. It is not always easy to determine whether a physical complaint is the cause or simply a lack of motivation (see p127–147).

Shared experiences
Simple games encourage a dog to exercise and are great fun for both owners and dogs.

Small, light dogs often remain very fit and active until late in life.

SIGNS YOUR DOG HAS OVEREXERTED ITSELF

→ Panting heavily

→ Labored, rapid breathing

→ Stopping often

→ Lying down

→ Lagging behind

→ Limping or avoiding certain kinds of movements

Q IS MY DOG IS GETTING AS MUCH EXERCISE AS IT SHOULD?

A You can easily tell by your dog's behavior whether it is getting too much or too little exercise. After a nice long walk and a rest or nap, it should be fit and active again. If the exertion was too much, some dogs will be completely exhausted afterward. Others cannot move about too well or will avoid specific types of movements for several days in a row. Usually, though, you can tell during the walk itself when you are asking your dog to do more than it can handle (*see above*).
Signs that a dog is getting too little exercise are restlessness or nervousness. Also, some into mischief by chewing things they should not, for example, or they bark excessively to get the attention and amusement they crave.

If an elderly dog does not get enough exercise, the suppleness of its joints deteriorates, and become stiff and inflexible. For this reason, challenge your dog. Demand that it gives you its utmost so that it stays in good physical condition and keeps a high endurance level for as long as possible. Many elderly and geriatric dogs are surprisingly resilient, and serious health limitations only crop up in advanced age.

A dog's breed also influences the type and amount of exercise it will need, and what its endurance limits will be when it is old. The extent to which dogs from very large, heavy breeds, such as Great Danes, need to be exercised declines much earlier on—and more visibly—than is the case with small, lively dogs such as Yorkshire Terriers.

CONSULTING YOUR VETERINARIAN

Whenever you bring your dog to the veterinarian, ask about its physical condition so you can better judge how much activity you can expect it to perform comfortably. Also consult with a veterinarian whenever you are unsure about your dog's physical capability or fitness level. In the following pages, we discuss many kinds of activities you can do with your dog. In general, if you and your dog would like to try out a new activity, such as swimming, and you have any doubts, first check with your veterinarian!

A visit to the animal hospital is also a must when your dog starts behaving oddly or moving in a different way than it normally does. Even when this just means your dog lags behind on a walk when it usually trots beside you, your veterinarian can find out if disease or pain is behind its behavior and, if needed, can start treating the problem (*see pp123–36*).

WALKS
and Hikes

By playing games and giving your dog tasks to do, you make walks interesting.

As a dog gets older, there is a change to the types of walks it can take and the distances it can cover.

With an older dog, it is not the amount of distance covered that is important but the length of time the dog is active and how long it is outside in the fresh air—activity itself is the goal (*see p21*). Taking walks with your dog gives a framework to its day and provides much-needed variety and stimulus to its body and mind. Even when you sometimes have to cajole your senior dog into going outside, you should never miss taking it on walks regularly for this reason.

It is important to exercise your dog on a regular basis. If your dog usually spends weekdays snoozing on the sofa, avoid taking it on forced marches on weekends. Your dog will not thank you. Hiking with your dog is a great experience when it is accustomed to such activity, handles it well, and if you pause often enough for a break—your elderly companion will appreciate being given a breather now and then. Many dogs often exceed their strength trying to keep up with their humans (*see chart left*).

SHOW IMAGINATION

Since most elderly dogs cannot handle long and tiring walks, take them for shorter walks along interesting pathways that offer variety instead. If there are fields and forests nearby, this is ideal (*see p24*). If there are none, you will have to drive your dog away for a walk as often as you can. Vary the paths you choose, distances walked, and types of terrain covered. Your dog will find something new to enjoy—and be kept busy—on each walk.

By playing games when you are underway you will also keep your dog busy. One game could be, for example, hiding its favorite toy or a food treat and letting it search for it. If your senior dog has never played this kind of game before, first let it watch while you hide the object. It will soon learn how to retrieve whatever you have hidden. You can also balance on fallen tree trunks with your dog, or look for mouse holes or chipmunk holes together and let your dog dig away at them where allowed. Nature offers many opportunities for varied and exciting walks.

Discovering something new
Walking along the same paths day in and day out is boring. It is much more fun to explore new paths together.

PLAYING IT SAFE

Very old, senile, hard-of-hearing, deaf, weak-sighted or blind dogs, have to be watched over carefully when they are running off leash since they might get lost. They may lack a sense of direction, miss linking up with you, and wander away. Some will join in with other groups of dogs or people, go off with them, and never find their way back home. To avoid such situations, think about using an extending leash on your dog (*see p92*).

The sheer joy of living
A senior dog with nothing to do? This should never happen! Elderly dogs relish an interesting challenge.

SPORT AND PLAY—
are these still possible?

Older dogs can definitely also take part in certain kinds of dog sports and special games.

Some types of sports are easily tailored to suit your elderly dog's abilities. Look over the various sport options open to your dog. Cross off the elements that are too grueling for it to do and pick out the ones that it can do—you now have an individually tailored fitness plan! As your dog grows older, however, you will very likely have to abandon one or more of these activities so pick out a few alternatives as early as possible. In the following pages we describe some of the ways you can keep your dog active and fit, and provide tips about what to watch out for.

SWIMMING

Since water supports its body, swimming will give your dog's joints a respite from bearing its body's entire weight and allow it to exercise its limbs freely. But, since swimming is very tiring, do not overdo it! Your dog might well need its strength to get home. Despite the advantages, do not try to force your dog to swim if it is water-shy. It will just freeze up if it is afraid. Avoid swift river currents, eddies, or steep banks. They are dangerous, and your dog can be drowned. An alternative to a swim in a lake, river or pond, is to take your dog to a dog swimming pool, especially in winter.

Thoroughly dry off your dog after it has been swimming and keep it moving so that it does not get chilled. A chill could be harmful to its muscles and joints, and also might result in a cold, bronchitis, or bladder infection.

Dogs belonging to breeds that were originally bred to work in the water, and related mixed breeds, usually love water and, even in winter, have no qualms about jumping in. Water-loving breeds include various types of Retrievers, Newfoundlanders, and Landseer Newfoundlanders.

Keeping up with a bicycle
Even on very long bike tours, your senior dogs can keep you company in a bicycle trailer.

KEEPING PACE WITH A BICYCLIST OR JOGGER

When it is not too hot outside, a dog in good condition can keep pace with a bicyclist, a jogger, or a speed-walker until quite late in life (see p21). Trotting along at an even pace on soft, springy surfaces is easy on the dog's joints, keeping it fit and its musculature strong. Avoid letting it run for long distances on concrete or asphalt paths. Adjust your speed to your dog's, and stop and wait if it has to slow down a bit now and then. Take the occasional break so that your dog has time to sniff alongside the path's edge, relieve itself, or have a drink of water.

If a dog is not allowed to run off the leash, good leash control is important in order to avoid damaging the dog's joints. If the dog continually pulls at the leash, it can strangle itself or compress its spine; the latter can happen even when it is wearing a harness.

Sometimes, due to wear and tear of its joints, or illness, you cannot allow your dog to run alongside you when you cycle for long distances. By placing your dog in a special bicycle trailer or basket, depending on its size, you can let it ride along with you. In this way, your dog accompanies you, can trot alongside you for smaller segments of the trip, and, for the rest of the time, simply enjoy the view.

Playing fetch
When you are considerate of its physical condition, your dog can often play fetch well into old age.

FETCHING

Although it looks quite easy, fetching things on command is very demanding. A great deal of training is needed before dogs can properly master this task, even for those bred to do this kind of work such as Retrievers. However, many other kinds of purebred and mixed breed dogs love to play fetch. It is up to you how your dog should carry out this command. For instance, should it watch as you throw a retrieving toy, see where it lands and then, on command, go and fetch it? Or should you hide the toy and let your dog find it and return it to you, with or without a little help from you? For older dogs, the best choice is usually to hide the retrieving toy (see p83).

Human help

When a dog has to overcome difficult obstacles during an agility trial, its human is responsible for giving it a sense of security and minimizing risks.

Exercising its powers of smell is a workout for its senses. Also, it will not have to speed up in a hurry to chase the thrown toy, or stop and start abruptly. Use a retrieval toy that is the appropriate size for your dog; it should not be too heavy or too large for the dog to carry easily.

AGILITY TRIALS

This demanding sport has become increasingly popular over the past few years. Dogs thoroughly enjoy the challenge and fun of agility training and the relaxed atmosphere of the training grounds. In this sport, using a combination of sight signals and verbal commands, a dog owner directs his or her dog over an obstacle course. The number and types of obstacles vary but generally include items such as a tire, weave poles, hurdles, a wall, an A-frame, a seesaw, a pause table, and a tunnel. Not only does the dog have to be in excellent physical and mental condition to participate in this sport, but the dog's owner also has to be enthusiastic and athletic. Jumping hurdles and weaving between poles can, however, be difficult, and also dangerous, for older dogs. However, you can still allow your dog to do agility training by adjusting the obstacle course to suit its age. Simply avoid all obstacles that call for leaps or could lead to sprains. You can also reduce the level of difficulty by, for example, increasing the distance between the slalom poles and significantly lowering the height of any hurdles. If you still want to take part regularly in agility competitions with your senior dog, and it is still healthy, you can always enter it into a veteran's category. For veterans,

Obstacles to suit a dog's age

Adjust agility course obstacles to suit the physical limitations of your senior dog. For example, use a wider see-saw, hang the tire lower, or lower the hurdles.

the height of the hurdles and the degree of slope of the A-frame is reduced, for example. Also, the time in which an older dog is required to complete the course is raised a notch. However, since agility trial rules on age, obstacle heights, and timing vary, check with local organizers to find out the best category for your senior dog.

CANINE FREESTYLE

In this sport, dog and dog owner move around each other and cut figures in time to music. These might involve the dog's standing on its hind legs, taking a long step with one stretched-out leg, weaving between its owner's legs or cutting a figure-eight around them, jumping over its owner's raised leg, through its arms, or over its back.

As is the case with agility training, when your dog gets on in years you will have to shorten and even eliminate some of the moves in Canine Freestyle such as leaps, pirouettes, and bends. However, there are very few moves left for old dogs, or dogs with health problems, to perform so perhaps you will to stop practicing the sport altogether. For this reason, Canine Freestyle—particularly the full program—is not suitable for all senior dogs.

Dexterity
Canine Freestyle is also fun for older dogs because, without stress, they learn easy tricks such as making a figure-eight around their owner.

PLAYING BALL, THROWING STICKS, FRISBEE

Most dogs enjoy all these activities. However, the sprints and quick stops these sports call for tax their joints, tendons, and muscles. Even when your senior dog is exceptionally fit, be very careful when letting it play these games. Also, since a dog can hurt its teeth or mouth when playing with hard objects, use only light sticks and Frisbees made out of plastic. Try not to hit the dog with the object you are throwing. To make the sport easier on your dog's joints, teach it to wait for your command before starting to run. This gives the dog time to better estimate the distance to the object thrown and to judge when it will have to apply the brakes.

DOG SHOWS

Attending dog shows is not a classic form of activity for dogs. However, it is important for us to mention it here. As in agility trials and other dog competitions, dog shows also have veteran categories. We would like to encourage all purebred dog owners whose dogs have good pedigrees to show their senior dogs as long as both owner and dog have fun doing so. Aside from the enjoyment factor, it is informative for dog breeders, interested observers, and future dog owners to see how well old dogs belonging to a given breed age. We think knowing this in advance is an important part of the decision-making process when you are choosing a purebred puppy.

MENTAL STIMULATION
—why is it crucial?

Training mind and body
Performing mental exercises keeps a dog's little gray cells active and fit.

Giving your dog the right amount of exercise is important to keeping it physically fit. However, most dogs are only fully engaged and well balanced when their mental powers are also stimulated.

Focusing, solving strategic problems or figuring out new situations, tires dogs out in a different way than does physical exercise. Perhaps you have experienced this yourself. Even though you are not performing a physically demanding job, but are "just" working at a desk job, you find yourself completely exhausted at the end of the day.

Even very active dogs can be tired out when they are mentally stimulated—without running around at all. And older dogs can be kept busy with mentally challenging tasks to make up for their diminishing physical powers.

Engaging in such demanding activities with your dog also has a positive side effect—your status is raised a notch in your dog's eyes since interesting adventures reinforce the bond between you and your canine friend (*see p88*). Here are some ideas for activities to do with your dog:

THE RIGHT MOOD

Make sure to train and play with your dog only when you are relaxed no matter what the goal, whether you are reinforcing commands it has already mastered, or teaching it new ones. If you are having a terrible day, feeling stressed, or do not have much time to spend, train or play with your dog at a later time. Your dog always knows when you are tense. Not only can it read your body language, but it can also smell the hormones your body produces when it is under stress such as cortisol. Even when you try to hide the fact that you are in a bad mood, your dog senses it and will not enjoy playing as much. Nor will it learn effectively. The opposite is also true: when your dog is feeling unwell because it is suffering from joint pain, for example, it will not absorb new things well or enjoy itself very much.

TRAINING GAMES

Build small learning units into every walk you take with your dog. Run through the basic commands your senior dog has already mastered. These will often be called upon during a walk in any case. For example, when a jogger or bicyclist is about to cross your path, you might have to give your

dog the command to sit. Train the dog for short periods of time only. In between, play games. Depending on whether you are walking in the

Be consistent
Even senior dogs have to obey commands and stick to the rules.

woods or not then you can consider adding some ground work, such as tracking or tasks requiring agility, to the exercises.

Sit and stay are easy commands to practice with your dog and you can vary the game according to the circumstances. At home, for example, roll a treat along the floor and only allow the dog to retrieve it on your command. In order to succeed, you must always dominate the game; your dog cannot be allowed to make decisions independently.

Some dogs get very bored practicing basic commands as they get older. New ideas and variety will be needed to keep them motivated and interested in working with you.

TRACKING

Dogs love using their noses, and their enthusiasm is matched only by their fatigue after a good spate of tracking. Following a scent has an advantage over many other activities in that it is a calm activity. Speed is not required, just focused searching. Also, you do not need complicated equipment for this activity, just, for example, bits of food to hide along the trail. Begin with short searches on easy trails. Then build up to a longer search and a reward your dog considers extremely desirable—such as a larger amount of food! You can also motivate a dog to follow a scent by using a special toy or ball, but food is usually the strongest motivator. Everyone can lay a tracking trail tailored to their dog's interests and needs, and trails can be laid on every sort of terrain, even in the house. Using a variety of locations will keep your dog interested and make sure that it gets a good workout. But do not just vary the terrain. Use different kinds of food rewards, from dry kibble to dog biscuits or small pieces of cheese or sausage. This is a good activity for a senior dog since, as its physical abilities decline, you can pick easier terrain and reduce the search radius to suit your dog.

Following a scent is tiring
Since tracking a scent is versatile and does not require speed, you can keep even very old dogs quite busy with this activity.

A DOG TALE

My twelve-year-old female Border Collie Jana loves herding sheep. But she is happiest when working the herd alone. If I give her too many orders, she gets stressed, as though she's trying to tell me "I see exactly what needs to be done and can do this all on my own— I don't need you to tell me what to do!" Jana especially enjoys helping train younger Border Collies to herd and to lead them. Since she has so much experience now, she hardly needs anyone to give her orders.

PLAYING AT HOME

There are many occasions when you will need to divert your dog by playing games with it at home. It might be that is raining outside, or it is too hot or cold, or your dog feels under the weather. Whatever the reason, there are many ways of arousing your dog's interest and keeping it amused.

- Fill a container, such as a cardboard box, with shredded paper and hide pieces of food inside for your dog to find. Or, using shredded paper, make a ball with food inside that your dog will roll around the floor until the desirable snacks fall out.
- Assign some of your dog's toys names and train it to find and bring you the right toys when you name them. As soon as it has learned the name of one toy, it is important to move on and train it to learn the next.
- Hide little treats in various rooms and let your dog search them out. At first, let your dog watch as you hide the treats. It will quickly learn what you are doing and then happily participate. Make the game more difficult by having your dog wait in another room while you hide the treats.
- Either you or another family member hides in another room. Ask the dog to find the missing person. Be prepared for a huge commotion when the dog locates the person!
- Step by step, teach your dog to search for, find, and bring you on command, common household objects such as the house keys, your wallet, your slippers, the newspaper, or the dog's leash.

Anyone ready for a game?
When the weather is bad, there are many ways of keeping your dog busy and amused inside the home.

Exercise your own imagination
Use a bit of fantasy when you want to create a game to keep your senior dog busy. For example, hide a dog biscuit or other delectable treat in a cardboard box or egg-carton filled with paper, or wrap up each treat in newspaper or old rags.

Gray and wise
Even when learning takes a bit longer—old dogs treasure new challenges.

A DOG TALE

LEARNING NEW THINGS

Learning is a lifelong activity—it is never too late to start, and it is never over. Even an elderly dog can adjust well to living with a new family and will come to learn a great many new things in the process (*see p64*).

Sometimes, even after a dog has been living with a family for several years, it will be necessary, or desirable, to train away bad habits or teach it to obey new commands, play new games, or learn new exercises.

Learning is not only great fun, it is also serves as a stimulus for the senior dog. After all, there is always praise and a reward for every exercise that has been done well! This is highly motivating. In contrast to younger dogs, training senior dogs takes a take a bit longer and will demand more patience from you. Dogs that have been challenged their entire lives, and that have always had new tasks to learn, learn more easily when they are older than dogs that never had to show their mettle.

My nine-year-old Dachshund Robbie first learned basic commands such as sit and stay when he was seven. But I didn't give him any special training! At the time, I was training Kato, my Munsterlander. Robbie simply learned along and surprised me by how swiftly he picked up the commands. I don't know whether he learned so quickly because he wanted to be included or because he noticed that there was always a treat after a command was mastered. Whatever the reason, he still loves training exercises and relishes every bit of praise and every reward, no matter how tiny.

BASIC TRAINING RULES

A dog can first enjoy privileges when it obeys the rules that its human has set.

You cannot train a dog properly if your approach is inconsistent. Even in the daily turbulence of family life, make sure to stick to the rules you have set and take action if they are not respected (*see p64*).

A dog will not learn well, and will suffer from stress, if it is subjected to an emotional roller-coaster because some things are permitted sometimes, but not always. For example, if you allow your dog to lie on the sofa once, but then chase it angrily away the next time because it is wet, it will not know what you want and become insecure.

Today, dog training has nothing to do with ensuring your dog is slavishly obedient to you. A well brought up dog can be allowed a great deal of freedom and it is enjoyable to help it learn new things. Lastly, there is no excuse—a dog definitely is not exempt from training just because it is old!

CLEAR HIERARCHIES

All animals that live in packs—and dogs are pack animals—have a well-defined place in the pack hierarchy. But, even though we human beings belong to a different species, the human-dog pack also needs a clearly defined structure that establishes, from the start, who is boss—who leads and who controls it. This has to be you, of course, not your dog. As a rule, both the highest-ranking human and the dominant canine in a pack are confident and calm leaders who usually have had a great deal of life experience. This experience is essential in helping them make decisions, fill the cabinet with food, avoid danger, and overcome risky situations. Remember that good leaders do not need to demonstrate their power by being loud, aggressive, or even violent. A pack's members can rely on their leader and trust the decisions it makes and the actions it takes.

Together through thick and thin When a dog has a confident human at its side, it can master even the most difficult situation calmly and competently.

Knowing its place

Another status-related aspect worth considering is the significant hierarchical difference existing between the highest-ranking and lowest-ranking members of a family group. When there are clearly defined differences in status, there is a high degree of mutual tolerance (*see p67*). This ensures harmonious and peaceful coexistence on a day-to-day basis. A dog does not think being of lower rank is a bad thing. Dogs do not lurk about behind-the-scenes waiting for an opportunity to challenge their leader and take over the pack as so many people assume they do. It is absolutely essential for a dog to know its exact status within the group. If it does not know where it stands, this might lead to misunderstandings and conflicts and the dog might attempt to resolve the situation on its own.

BUILDING A BOND

If your elderly dog has been with you for several years, then you already will have established a stable social relationship with it, something you will have to work at achieving with a new senior dog. A prerequisite for achieving a good relationship is that a bond exists between you and your dog. To picture this bond, try to imagine that there is an invisible elastic band linking you and your dog—a mental link, as it were, between two partners. Dogs look to their social partners

LEADERSHIP ROLE

When several dogs live under the same roof, they create a hierarchy among themselves. It is interesting to observe if and how the status of an individual animal changes as it gets older. Some keep their status as the dominant canine without ever being challenged. Others are happy to relinquish this role to a younger member of the pack. On occasion, dogs will fight and even wound each other during a transfer of power. To make it easier for the dogs to create a new order, the human should accept the hierarchy they have established but always remain the confident leader at the head of the pack.

A great team
When the bond is right, few words are needed to understand each other.

for their emotional well-being. Both you and your dog will adjust to each another and make compromises. For the dog, this can mean coming when called, sitting on command, and not pulling on its leash during a walk. For you, the human, this can mean feeding the dog, paying the veterinarian, taking a walk with your dog even when it is cold and rainy outside, or cleaning the floor uncomplainingly when your dog has diarrhea. Bonding entails communicating with and paying attention to each other, even when there are many distractions. There is mutual respect; each knows and caters to the other's needs, and each has faith in the other. When you and your dog have achieved a solid bond, you will both enjoy doing activities together and take pleasure in each other's company.

"Bonding entails communicating with and paying attention to each other."

Creating a bond

Playing interesting games and having new experiences together can help create a strong bond between you and your dog. Motivating a dog with food treats—giving it tasks it is "paid" for will also help. A good relationship needs time to develop and grow, and some dogs definitely make it easier for their humans than others. Whatever your approach is, know what your dog considers appealing and important. Building these things into your daily routine increases your own status and promotes the relationship. The more attractive you are to the dog, the stronger its bond to you will be.

However, in certain situations, the bonding process can be blocked or even destroyed if you do not give your dog enough mental or physical challenges, for example. Another problem arises when there is a large discrepancy in the way you have bonded to each other, for example, when you are much more attached to your dog than it is to you.

A feeling of security
Trust is an important building-block in the relationship between you and your dog.

Trust

A further element in the relationship between human and canine is trust. To your dog, you, the human, are like a rock in the floodwaters, offering it security and safety in new or dangerous situations. Trust is fragile. It can be shattered easily. For example, if your dog experiences great fear in a given situation and links you with the situation, trust is broken. It is easy enough to tell just by body contact if your dog trusts you or not. Does your dog visibly enjoy being stroked by you and does it relax completely when you pet it? Or, if you bend over when you are patting it, get really close to it, or hug it, does it show hesitancy?

EXPERT ADVICE

If you have not had very much experience training dogs, or are uncertain about what to do in a specific situation, you should consider enrolling in a good dog school, just as you would when any other behavioral problems crop up. Along with practical exercises and tips, professional help will let you find your own way to deal with your senior dog. However, not every kind of behavior can be corrected through training. Some forms of behavior will have entrenched themselves over the years, almost like data burned onto a hard drive. But even here it is a good idea to seek advice in order to confidently deal with the quirk or fault, and not to reinforce the problem. There is no patent recipe in dog training—no one method that is valid for every dog. Each dog is different, every human being too, and the training has to suit both so that it is consistently implemented and is successful. A good trainer will draw on various training methods and put together various segments from each to create a tailor-made plan for you and your dog.

Deciding what is important
Excessive barking can be very annoying. On the other hand, a vocal dog keeps away unwanted visitors.

SETTING PRIORITIES—WHAT IS IMPORTANT TO YOU?

When an elderly dog that never has learned the basic commands moves in with you, you can still teach it the most important ones. Not every dog needs to be taught the full program. Set priorities. At first, only teach it commands that are necessary and helpful to the daily routine. Training your dog to obey a command that would be just nice to have your dog know but is not really essential, such as bringing your slippers, should be postponed to a later date.

Is your senior dog already suffering from health problems, such as arthritis of the joints or a hip ailment? Then, out of consideration for it, consider skipping some commands such as sit or stay, or allow it more time to respond to commands or perform difficult tasks.

Nice but unnecessary
Having your dog bring you the daily newspaper is a wonderful trick, but it is not essential for day-to-day living.

LEARNING IN THE RIGHT WAY

TRAINING PLAN

- 3 or, at the most, 5 times a day train for 5 to 10 minutes
- Divide difficult exercises into small segments
- Train new commands without any distractions
- Reinforce already learned commands through repetition
- Reinforce already learned commands with distractions

A DOG TALE

My female Ibizan Podenco Hound Lena moved in with me when she was eight. She did not know any basic commands, but was a calm dog that fit right into her new life in a new environment and easily adjusted to my daily routine. She lay down without prompting when she was relaxed, and walking her on a leash was no problem. When I trained her, I limited myself to teaching her only two commands, sit and come after running off-leash. No other commands were needed to handle her properly.

Many factors influence how a dog learns to respond to commands. Hold training sessions often, train in increments and keep the lessons short. This is much better than lengthy training once or twice a week.

All dogs learn through success and failure but each dog responds differently to obedience training. Some need more time than others to absorb new commands and only learn after much repetition; others learn quickly. You will have to devise your own plan as to how to best motivate your dog to work with you during training, and to enjoy itself in the process. There are many ways to motivate your canine companion. The most commonly used motivators are food and treats, praise, a short pat, a favorite toy, or a game you play together after training. When you train your dog, you should be calm and relaxed (*see p82*). Pick a quiet location with no distractions, such as the hallway of your house, to start training a new command. Once your dog responds reliably in that location, move on to other locations with more distractions and reinforce the commands there. Later, on a regular basis, repeat even the most basic commands that your dog has already mastered. Make sure it carries them out properly, and correct any mistakes immediately.

PRAISE AND DISCIPLINE

In our opinion, there are two key elements in dog training—positive and negative reinforcement of a desired behavior. Dogs learn from the consequences of their actions. If they link an action with something positive, such as being praised, given a delicious food reward, or patted, they will naturally want to repeat the action—its behavior has been positively reinforced. On the other hand, if your dog associates an action with an unpleasant act, such being disciplined, it will try to avoid this activity in future—its behavior has been negatively reinforced. Whether or not you praise or discipline your dog, do so immediately. If your dog misbehaves and even half a minute elapses before you discipline it, it will not be able to make the link between the two actions. The same is true for praise; giving an immediate reward is important to achieving the results you want.

Praise and rewards

Using praise and rewards as often as possible, try to motivate your dog so that it comes to enjoy behaving in the way you want it to. Rewards animate a dog to happily work with you during its training. Reward your dog generously when you start training it to respond to a new command. However, as your dog begin mastering the new command, incrementally reduce the rewards. Graduate to simple praise, and, finally, do nothing whatsoever. Your dog's response should now be a matter of course and need no reinforcement. Even so, later on, you should give your dog the occasional reward when it has responded well to a command in order to keep training exciting.

Training aids
There are many ways of encouraging a dog to work with you during training. Discover what kind of motivation works best for your dog.

Food and delicious treats

Toy

Useful for every dog owner, a treat bag

Q AT HOME, MY DOG DOES NOT CARRY OUT THE COMMANDS IT LEARNED IN DOG TRAINING SCHOOL. WHY?

A Dogs link what they have learned with the person, place, or other circumstances they have experienced in training. For this reason, it is important to train your dog in many different places. Doing part of your dog's training where it later will be called upon to respond, such your local park, is an especially good idea.

Discipline

Unfortunately, it is practically impossible to train a dog just by using positive reinforcement. Some kinds of behavior can be improved simply by ignoring the dog. In order to properly ignore a dog, do not look at it, speak to it, or even touch it. The goal is to reduce the undesirable behavior or eliminate it altogether. But be careful—even the simple act of sending your dog out of the room, for example, means you are paying attention to it or condoning its behavior.

Ignoring a dog is not always a strong enough disciplinary measure when you are training it. Now and then you will need to use clear commands to stop it from doing something such as digging up a houseplant in front of your eyes. Stop signals can take various forms and can range in sharpness. They can include a harsh "no," or use of dominant body language such as bending over the dog, bumping it, or using a muzzle grip. It depends on your dog's character how often these kinds of corrective measures might be called for.

MUZZLE HOLD

Sometimes, in certain circumstances, a dog will clamp down on another dog's muzzle as way of stopping undesirable behavior. Mothers control obstreperous puppies in this way. This is a very strong and powerful tool that you can use to control your dog when it is misbehaving. However, do not use this grip on a regular basis, or for small misdemeanors! It is especially difficult to apply this grip promptly and correctly to small, lively, dogs, or dogs that are behaving aggressively. Do not attempt it if there is any chance you cannot apply the grip immediately or in the proper way.

However you decide to deal with the canine miscreant, make sure your reaction is appropriate to the misdemeanor. Sometimes less is more. You should never hit the dog or use any other kind of physical punishment to correct its behavior. This will only result in destroying any trust that your dog has placed in you!

TRAINING AIDS

There are many aids on the market that can help when you are training your dog—but only if they are used in the right way. In general, after they have been used successfully, they should be phased out. If you intend to use training aids we recommend that you enlist the help of a dog trainer because using them in the wrong way might actually harm your dog. A trainer can advise you whether or not you will even need to use special aids to train your dog.

Leashes

Leashes used in training vary in length and thickness, depending on a dog's age, size, and training level. For example, if your dog is large, a thin nylon leash might cut into your hand when you try to stop your dog. When you first start training, a shorter leash makes it easier to control the dog. Later, graduate to a longer leash, such as an extending leash, which will give your dog freedom of movement but still allow you to control it.

Whistles

Dogs have to be trained to respond to whistles. Our favorite is an audible buffalo horn whistle. With a silent dog whistle we never know for sure if it is working or not. It might be blocked up by dirt, for example, or it is working and the dog is simply ignoring it. Whistles have the advantage that they convey a clear command to your dog without any of your own emotions being transmitted.

Leashes come in various lengths, materials, and thicknesses.

Dog whistles allow signals to be transmitted over a great distance.

Metal whistle

Buffalo horn whistle

Head halters

A halter provides an excellent way of controlling a dog. When the dog lunges forward, the halter's nose band tightens, pulling the dog's jaws shut and its head down. By facilitating communication between dog and human, halters make it easier to train dogs to the leash. But, even after basic training has been completed, using a halter all the time is the best way to control some dogs. This has nothing to do with a dog's size but is usually rather a matter of its strength-of-will. For any dog though, it is not a sign of weakness if, even after basic training, you occasionally have to put its halter on!

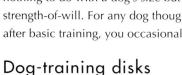

Nose band

Halter lead ring

Dog-training disks

These are saucer-shaped metal disks that make a unique nose. They are negative reinforcers. A dog needs to be trained gradually before it responds to them properly and stops the undesirable behavior. A third party, never a dog's owner, should carry out this type of training, and only the most undesirable kinds of behavior should be corrected using disks.

Disks

Clicker training

Clickers allow you to instantly create a link in your dog's mind between the clicker and a particular act. If the dog is properly clicker trained, it will very soon understand that a sound signal—the click—signals approval of a certain type of behavior and it can expect a tasty reward immediately afterward. The underlying principle is rewarding desirable behavior and ignoring undesirable behavior immediately. It is, however, impossible to use a clicker to train a dog not to do something.

"The underlying principle of clicker training is rewarding desirable behavior and ignoring undesirable behavior."

Aside from training basic commands, clickers can also be used to train dogs to do tricks or carry out tasks. They are used to train assistance dogs and service dogs to perform tasks such as lifting and fetching specific items or turning switches on or off. But elderly dogs, too, can be kept busy and content learning tricks with a clicker. And, if they cannot move around too much due to their age, you can devise various way of amusing them using clicker training, even in the home. Many dogs show enormous enthusiasm for this training aid and, amazingly quickly, come to understand the links between clicks and rewards.

Training clicker

TIPS ON HOW TO TRAIN BLIND OR DEAF DOGS

Dealing with dogs that have seeing or hearing difficulties is, at first, a great challenge for their owners. But when they have come to terms with the situation, such impairments do not normally present a significant problem in everyday life. A dog usually adjusts very well to a declining faculty. In fact, it can take its owner a long time even to realize that the dog is no longer seeing or hearing very well and react accordingly.

One basic mistake owners of such dogs make is to spoil them since, after all, they are such pitiable, handicapped creatures. However, the best thing to do is to treat them as you would all other canines. Give them a regular routine and firm rules, and you will give them the sense of security they need.

Senior dogs with a disability can be trained to react to alternative commands and kept busy. Here, snapping fingers indicate the right way.

DEAF DOG	BLIND DOG
Reward visual contact often using appealing treats	Reward it often with an appealing treat when it comes
Give unequivocal and distinct hand signals	Use clearly distinguishable voice commands
Make sure your body language can be read clearly	Make sure that the voice command is not used constantly in normal speech such as no and good
Use facial expressions: → say commands at the same time as you signal them → look happy when you praise your dog → look angry when it has done something wrong	Use clicker training to train your dog to learn new commands (see p93)
Introduce new hand signals such as "thumb's up" Use other deaf and dumb language signals as needed	Use special noises such as clicking with your tongue to gain the dog's attention, or snapping your fingers to control it

HAND SIGNALS AND VOICE COMMANDS

Dogs can be trained to respond to both hand signals and voice commands. Training dogs to respond to both types of signals when they are fairly young can come in very handy. At the least, you will always have an alternative. And, if in later years your dog becomes deaf or blind, you can shift from hand signals to voice commands—or vice versa—as the situation requires. But it is important to teach a dog both types of commands before its senses deteriorate. On this page, we briefly demonstrate some of the hand signal equivalents for voice commands you can use:

Sit
Hold your index finger at breast level and point upward.

Stay
Stretch out your arm at breast height with your palm facing outward and hand held upright. Use this signal every time you want your dog to wait for you.

Lie down
Extend your hand flat and parallel to the ground.

Come
Hold your hand at chin level. With your palm facing you, bend your fingers toward the palm's surface.

Heel
Hit your hand gently on the outside of your upper left thigh when your dog heels on your left-hand side. Hit your hand on the outside of your upper right thigh when your dog heels on the right.

Go
Stretch your arm out fully and raise it above eye-level. With your palm facing downward, point straight ahead.

NUTRITION

KNOWING HOW MUCH and what kind of food a dog eats every day is crucial to being able to determine whether it is properly nourished or not. When a dog begins to age and age-related changes become evident, its diet will have to be adjusted accordingly.

By feeding your dog a well-balanced diet tailored to its specific needs you will help slow down the onset of the aging process, and also mitigate its effects and extent. However, age-related symptoms that have already surfaced cannot be undone. Key to a dog's good health in old age is that it has maintained its ideal weight throughout life. Therefore keeping your dog slim and trim is the best way to improve its life expectancy and quality of life. Obesity, on the other hand, always has a negative effect!

Good nutrition can prevent illness and slow down the effects of aging, but you will also have to change the way you feed your dog if it contracts an acute or chronic illness. Aged dogs, especially, might need to follow a new diet when they become ill. Sometimes a new diet will have to be followed for just a short time, sometimes forever. Your veterinarian will advise you what to do when your senior dog becomes ill, and suggest the best diet for your dog.

METABOLIC CHANGES
and their effects

In a dog's body, chemical processes cause foodstuffs to be broken down, transformed, absorbed, and, finally, excreted. This is known as the metabolic process.

Illnesses occur when a dog's metabolism is not working properly. Changes in its hormonal balance, degenerative changes to various organs, and a decline in the amount of physical activity it performs—all these things can influence a dog's organism and cause its metabolism to slow. Also, decreased metabolic activity causes a dog's body to change as it ages. The number of fat cells in its body increases, and muscle mass decreases, altering the ratio of body fat to muscle fat. This is why a dog's total energy needs decrease by about 30 percent during the last third of its life. Your dog needs less food when it is older and for this reason it is absolutely essential to reduce the number of calories you feed it in this phase of its life.

A nice break now and then
Elderly dogs are not as active as they were when younger and require a calorie-reduced diet to keep them as healthy as possible.

STOMACH AND DIGESTIVE SYSTEM

As a dog ages, its digestive system changes. It no longer processes and absorbs the nutrients in its food as well as it once did. Tooth decay or badly functioning salivary glands can also lead to poor food metabolization—food is chewed less or salivary enzymes that break food down are not as plentiful. Since a dog's digestive system is extremely sensitive, it can react to even a small, temporary change in its diet with diarrhea. On the other hand, when dogs are older, their large intestines are less active and this can result in constipation.

Chewed food mixed with saliva reaches the dog's stomach through the esophagus

In the stomach, gastric acid and digestive enzymes help prepare food for absorption by the intestines

Key nutrients are absorbed in the small intestine

A dog's stomach can hold large quantities of food. However, when a dog is old, smaller and more frequent meals are easier to digest.

ENERGY

As a dog ages, its energy level declines. How, and when, is unique to each dog.

Dogs that lose their vitality at an early age are usually less energetic than others as young adult dogs. Size is also a factor. If a dog weighs about 88lb (40 kilos), its energy level can be expected to decline by the time it is five or six years old.

Energy is derived from proteins, fat, and carbohydrates. By burning various kinds of food in a process known as oxidation, the body releases energy. How much energy is released depends on how digestible the food is. A dog's body absorbs a large amount of the nutrients in food that is easy to digest. When a dog does not get enough energy, it loses weight, its energy level diminishes, and its body functions deteriorate. It might not even be able to maintain the right body temperature when its energy level is extremely low. When a dog is fed too much, it has been given more energy than it can use. Excess energy is stored as fat and leads to canine obesity.

Very lively dogs
require much more food energy than easygoing ones.

PROTEINS

Old dogs, in particular, need high-quality nutrients that are easy to digest and served in portions tailored to their individual needs. The aging process causes muscle mass to shrink. But the protein reserves that a dog calls on in times of stress and illness will shrink too when a dog does not eat enough protein to maintain them.

Digestibility

Digestive enzymes break down easily digestible proteins into shorter amino acid chains. These are then absorbed by the intestinal wall into the bloodstream and transported to the body's organs.

Plant proteins are digested much less efficiently by dogs than animal proteins. Everything that cannot be broken down is expelled in a dog's excrement. But undigested proteins remain too long in the large intestine and decompose. Bad-smelling flatulence is the result. Easy-to-digest proteins are found in lamb, fish, chicken, and cooked chicken gizzards, for example. The protein source and amount that is just right for your dog depends on many factors such as how well your dog tolerates it. If you are unsure about the kind of food that is best for your dog, consult with your veterinarian.

Obesity
If your dog is getting pudgy, it is high-time for more activity and food better suited to your dog's needs.

A gleaming coat
Essential fatty acids help your dog
grow a thick and healthy coat.

Biological Value

A protein is considered to have a high biological value when its individual components—amino acids—can be broken down and exploited optimally by an organism. The body's kidneys—which help detoxify the body—excrete unused amino acids, or amino acids that do not match the body's own proteins in the form of urine. When this occurs in great amounts, the kidneys can become overworked. Sources of protein that are of high biological value are chicken organs, chicken, lamb and fish.

FAT

Fats are essential to a dog's being well nourished. They are a concentrated form of energy and should be easily digestible, such as pork and chicken fat. Fats deliver long-lasting energy to the body that is easy for it to store. But fat, too, should be of high quality in order to provide a dog with the essential fatty acids and the fat soluble vitamins A, D, E, and K that it needs. Since a dog's metabolism cannot produce essential fatty acids, these must be supplied by its diet. Your dog's coat and skin, for example, will be healthier when it is fed fatty acids.

You should also make sure your dog's food contains an optimal ratio of omega-6 to omega-3 fatty acids, which are polyunsaturated fats. Not only do these kinds of fatty acids help give your dog a healthy coat and skin but they will also help against inflammation.

CARBOHYDRATES

Chemically speaking, carbohydrates can be divided into those producing single sugars, such as glucose and fructose, and multiple—or complex—sugars (polysaccharides), such as starches and cellulose. Carbohydrates have the advantage of being transformed into quick energy. But dogs do not really need to be fed carbohydrates since they can readily obtain quick energy eating fat and protein.

"Fats are a concentrated source of food energy and should be easily digestible."

As dogs became domesticated over time, they were fed carbohydrates because these were an inexpensive source of food energy. Today, however, nutritionists know that some types of carbohydrates, such as the cellulose contained in fiber-rich foods, are very good for a dog's digestive system. A diet with a well-balanced fiber content gives a dog a feeling of satiation, provides bulk needed for normal stool passage, and helps a dog's digestive tract remain healthy.

VITAMINS AND MINERALS

Dogs, just like humans, need vitamins and minerals to be able to function properly. Usually a dog is well supplied with these when it is fed the right kind of manufactured dog food. However, if you make your own dog food, you might have to add some kinds of supplements so that it has a well-balanced diet (*see p104*). But, even if you think your dog's diet is lacking something, you should never strike off on your own and add minerals, vitamins, or trace elements to its food. First, discuss with your veterinarian whether or not supplements are called for.

THE RIGHT DIET

There is no single recommendation as to which type of food is best appropriate for all dogs.

The important thing is that your dog tolerates its normal food well and is getting a balanced diet. Signs that its diet needs adjusting are production of a large amount of feces, heavy flatulence, scaly skin, or a dull coat. For any questions that you have or problems that arise in regard to your dog's nutrition, consult your veterinarian.

WATER

Water is also essential for dogs; they need it to maintain all their vital functions. How much fresh drinking water a dog needs depends on several factors, such as the amount it is exercised, the weather, and what kind of food it is fed—wet or dry. When your dog suddenly starts drinking more water than usual, ask your veterinarian to find out why. Many fairly common diseases that crop up when dogs get old are accompanied by increased thirst. These include inflammation of the uterus in bitches, or diabetes and kidney disease.

A raised food bowl is a great boon for larger dogs to eat from, especially those with arthritis or spinal disease.

Do not just feed your dog meat; dogs need a balanced diet in order to remain healthy and fit.

FEEDING OPTIONS

DRY FOOD	CANNED FOOD	HOMEMADE FOOD	FRESH FOOD
High-quality premium product*	High-quality premium product*		
Single food source with a good balance between nutrients and the amount of energy provided	Single or supplementary food source with about 70–80% water	Must be tailored to the dog's needs	Must be tailored to the dog's needs
Practical—especially when traveling	Food in an opened can spoils easily when it is hot	Is more time-consuming to prepare and keep	Is more time-consuming to prepare and store
Nutritional composition constant	Nutritional composition constant	Needs to be well balanced	Needs to be well balanced
Medium acceptance level	High acceptance level	High acceptance level	High acceptance level
Denatured through commercial preparation	Denatured through commercial preparation	Some of the nutrients and vitamins are lost in the cooking process	Fresh preparation, natural. Nutrients may be less readily available to the body
Different kinds available (various protein sources and for a variety of needs) 	Different kinds available (various protein sources and for a variety of needs) 	Requires dedication and detailed knowledge about different dietary require-ments 	Requires dedication and detailed knowledge about different dietary requirements 

* High-quality premium products are distinguished by carefully selected, well-balanced ingredients that are always consistent.

THE AMOUNT OF FOOD A DOG NEEDS DEPENDS ON:

→ Its age

→ Its sex and whether or not it has been neutered

→ Its activity level and its temperament

→ Its breed or type

→ Where it lives and how it is kept (i.e., house or apartment, outside or inside)

→ The amount of energy its food contains

WHAT TYPE OF FOOD?

It is your decision as to what type of food—commercially prepared or homemade—you feed your dog. The above chart shows the most common feeding choices and the differences between them.

HOW OFTEN, HOW MUCH?

By eating several smaller meals each day, a senior dog is able to digest its food more effectively and is not as hungry between meals. Divide your dog's daily food rations into three portions and spread them out over the day. Always try to feed your dog at the same times each day, and do not deviate more than an hour or two from the schedule—some senior dogs react to irregular feeding times with digestive problems. Your dog's food should always be served at room temperature, never straight from the refrigerator!

TREATS BETWEEN MEALS

Each treat you give your dog, even during training, must be counted as part of its daily food ration. Dog owners often underestimate the number of treats they give their dogs each day and the calories that are in them. Many snacks are completely unsuited for senior dogs. Cross products off your shopping list that are sweet and sugary and full of fat. Treats that have few calories and are easily digestible include beef chews, rawhide chews, dried lung, or dried meat strips. Delicious and inexpensive alternatives to these commercially prepared treats are pieces of carrots, apples, and celery, and rusks.

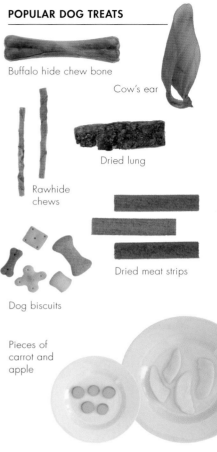

POPULAR DOG TREATS

Buffalo hide chew bone

Cow's ear

Dried lung

Rawhide chews

Dog biscuits

Dried meat strips

Pieces of carrot and apple

Tasty rewards
Make your dog earn the tastiest treats, too.

SWITCHING DOG FOOD

Never change something that works well, so avoid changing a dog's food unless it is absolutely necessary! If you have to change your dog's food—from dry to moist food, for example—do so gradually over the course of seven to ten days. Bit by bit, mix small quantities of the new food into your dog's regular food. Increase the amount each day until, after about a week,

LOVING YOUR DOG WITH TOO MUCH FOOD

Showing a dog affection does not mean feeding it until it is as round as a bowling ball! The length and quality of a dog's life is shortened by obesity! A dog should live a life appropriate for dogs, not humans. Find other ways to have fun with and enjoy your dog. Amuse it with puzzles and walks, pet it, and give it special massages. When you want to give it a treat remember that less is more.

Switching slowly
Changing a dog's food should take place slowly. If your dog is now eating more dry food, it will need to drink more.

you have made a complete switch. If your dog gets digestive problems from its new diet, take a couple of steps back and introduce the new food even more slowly. Your patience will be rewarded.

SUPPLEMENTS

If you are already feeding your dog a premium, complete, dry food, it is getting all the nutrients it needs for a well-balanced diet. No supplements are needed. Dogs that are fed homemade food, or are suffering from health problems or illness, benefit from being fed some supplements. Before going this route, discuss with your veterinarian what would be best for your dog. Here is a small selection of supplements:

WHAT?	USE?
Green-lipped mussel extract	It protects and regenerates joint cartilage. Contains glucosamine and chondroitin. Good for dogs suffering from hip or elbow dysplasia or arthritis.
Evening primrose oil and safflower oil	Essential fatty acids are good for the skin and coat.
Salmon oil	Contains a high amount of omega-3 and omega-6 fatty-acids. It is an anti-inflammatory and is good for the skin and coat.
Grated apple	Contains pectin, which regulates digestion.
Grated carrots	Help against diarrhea.
Healing herbs and plants	Hawthorn, for example, helps with heart problems; caraway and fennel seeds help reduce flatulence.

High-quality oils provide essential fatty acids

Salmon oil is also available in capsule form

SPECIAL DIETS

Senior dogs are prone to suffer from digestive problems. Depending on the breed, being fed later than usual, an unaccustomed treat, an exciting visitor, or a change in daily routine can cause minor stomach upsets and digestive problems. When this happens, feed your dog light foods that are easy to digest. These include boiled rice mixed with cooked chicken, fish with all bones carefully removed, low fat curd cheese and cottage cheese. Switch back slowly to your dog's normal diet.

Cottage cheese is very easy for dogs to digest.

DIETS

If your dog is suffering from an age-related illness, you might have to put it on a special diet temporarily, perhaps even permanently. Regular dog food does not satisfy the dietary needs of a dog that has an acute or chronic illness. Commercially prepared dog foods that have been designed to help fight various diseases are available. They have been designed by veterinarians, and are usually available only from them, since—just as for prescription drugs—an exact diagnosis is required before it can be used. If you would like to prepare your own special diet food for your invalid dog, first consult with your veterinarian and inform yourself by reading specialist literature. In the chart below, we provide information about a few types of diets.

HOW WELL-FED IS YOUR DOG?

At regular intervals, weigh your dog and write down the results for later comparison. You also can check its nutritional health just by feel. To do this, simultaneously run your fingers along both sides of your dog's chest to feel its ribs. You should be able to feel them easily. If you can also distinguish a waist, then the dog's weight is just fine. You can tell a dog is under-nourished if its ribs, lumbar vertebrae and pelvic bones clearly show. An overweight dog has a definite fat layer and usually you can hardly distinguish a waist. Exceptions are very slim dog breeds, such as Whippets, or very strong and sturdy dogs, such as Molossers.

A DOG TALE

Two years ago, during a routine examination, Charly, our ten-year-old Jack Russell mix, was diagnosed with diabetes. Since that day, he's been on a special diet, and thankfully the disease has been kept under control. Even better, we don't have to inject Charly with insulin! So that it stays this way, it is very important that we strictly follow the feeding instructions.

Weight control
Large dogs can be weighed at the veterinarian's.

DIETS FOR ...	REASON/CHANGE
Kidney disease	To reduce the amount of toxic by-products produced when the body processes proteins (urea), the intake of protein and phosphorus is reduced. This special food contains high-value protein in small quantities.
Liver disease	Undesirable metabolic by-products that overwork the liver need to be reduced. The diet food has to be easy to digest, rich in carbohydrates, and low in copper. This diet contains high-value protein.
Inflammation of the pancreas	Here, a fat-reduced diet, rich in easily digestible proteins, is called for. Only certain kinds of carbohydrates and few, carefully selected, fats are appropriate.

EATING GRASS

Almost all dogs eat grass every now and then. They often graze when their tummies are rumbling and gurgling. Some dogs vomit afterward, some do not, but most seem to benefit in some way. Even the Swiss herbalist Pastor Künzle (1857–1945) observed that dogs ate couch grass (also known under other names such as quickgrass and dog's grass) when they were suffering from digestive problems. Tea made from couch grass root is used a home remedy for stomach and intestinal problems. Your dog knows best—whenever it feels the urge, let it eat grass.

CANINE OBESITY

The owners of aged neutered dogs are often faced with the problem that their canine companions are too fat (see p105). Obesity reduces a dog's mobility and it moves less—a vicious circle. But being overweight does not just have a negative impact on a dog's physical fitness. Carrying excess weight is hard on its joints, circulation, and can lead, for example, to diabetes. There is more risk when the dog has to be given anesthesia. This is why it is important to help your dog regain its trim figure. The first line of attack against obesity is increasing a dog's activity as much you can while taking its limitations into account. Taking your dog on more walks will help (see p77). At the same time, adjust its diet. However, by no means should you simply reduce the quantity of food you feed it, or even set it on a fasting diet, since a lack of nutrients can make your dog sick!

Little thieves
make good on every opportunity that comes their way to snap up a tasty tid-bit.

In an unobserved moment, the daring rascal sneaks up on its prey and wolfs it down.

For this reason, do not leave food that your dog can reach unattended.

If the dastardly deed is done before you return, reduce the day's food ration by a small amount.

When your dog is only slightly overweight—up to ten percent heavier than its ideal body weight—you can feed it light dog food, also called low-calorie food. It is low in fat and, instead, contains more carbohydrates. A really overweight dog needs to be treated by a veterinarian, who will reduce its weight under controlled circumstances. Your dog will be set on a special diet, and its health and progress monitored as it gradually slims down to its

To serve the right amount each time, draw a line on a glass or use a measuring-cup

ideal body weight. There are a few simple ways to help maintain your dog's ideal weight. Precisely measure out your dog's food at each feeding time. Use the same measure each time. Cut out all the snacks, or count them as part of the daily food ration. Make sure your dog cannot wolf up food you set out for other animals living in your household, such as dry cat food, or sneak food from plates. All your family members, especially the children, will have to follow these rules in order to control your dog's weight successfully.

WHEN YOUR DOG IS UNDERWEIGHT

Sometimes it can happen that very old dogs suffer from extreme weight loss—up to one-fifth of their body weight. There are many reasons for this, such as loss of appetite, problems with their sense of smell (*see above*), food that is not easily processed by their bodies, mouth and dental problems that make it difficult, painful, or even impossible for them to eat, as well organ disease.

Any dog that loses weight steadily, or suddenly refuses its food, should be taken to the veterinarian to find out why. If there is an underlying illness, it needs treating. At the same time, after consultation with the veterinarian, the dog should be fed an easy-to-digest, calorie-rich food and possibly an appetite stimulator. It is extremely important to switch to feeding smaller portions more often throughout the day. In serious cases, artificial food will be recommended.

WHEN THE TASTE IS GONE

A dog's senses decline as it becomes older, and its sense of taste can also diminish. Since smell and taste are closely linked, food that no longer smells as good no longer tastes as good. As a result, your dog's appetite might become poorer. To counteract this, try warming your dog's food briefly in the microwave or adding warm water to it. This will intensify its aroma. You can also mix in low-salt vegetable broth, low-fat cottage cheese, or low-fat yogurt instead of warm water. Some dogs also respond well when they are fed by hand.

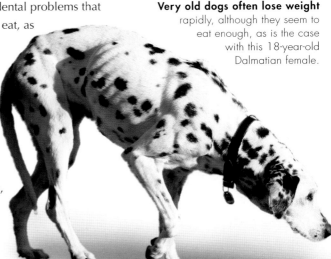

Food fed by hand often tastes better to underweight and sick dogs

Very old dogs often lose weight rapidly, although they seem to eat enough, as is the case with this 18-year-old Dalmatian female.

ROUTINE CARE

ELDERLY DOGS ARE COMPLETELY dependent on their owners to care for them, and need more assistance than younger dogs. As dogs age, they begin to suffer from numerous mild complaints and illnesses, from the tips to their noses to the ends of their tails.

Giving a senior dog attentive routine care prevents many of these complaints from arising, saves the dog much suffering, and improves its quality of life. Since many of the preventive measures that can be taken cost only time, routine care saves every dog owner money down the line. And too, regular care means that you quickly will spot changes in your dog that serve as warning signals. Illnesses will therefore be caught earlier, and treatment will often be less invasive and costly. Through regular care, even the unpleasant body odor that sometimes accompanies old dogs will be reduced, or even avoided entirely.

The loving attention you give your dog when caring for it is also like a pat on the dog's soul. Caring for your senior dog is not just a matter of attending to its appearance, it also, and more importantly, means seeing to its well-being.

COAT AND SKIN CARE

A dog's coat is a mirror of its health and, by the same token, of the attention its owner pays to it. The wrong kind of diet, internal organ disease, and metabolic problems cause many skin and coat problems.

When a dog's coat shows changes—when it becomes dull or brittle, or thins out—do not just assume this is a normal sign of aging. Find out why. Unfortunately, not all old dogs are groomed as thoroughly as they should be. When a dog's fur mats up, the microclimate of the underlying skin is destabilized. Infections can arise more easily and external parasites such as ticks lurk undiscovered. However, when a dog's coat is cared for properly and groomed regularly, skin changes are spotted quickly. If necessary, take your dog to the veterinarian, who will find out the reason and provide the proper treatment.

Use regular grooming
as an opportunity for checking skin and fur and discovering any changes quickly.

ALL ABOUT COAT AND SKIN

A dog's skin consists of two layers—the **epidermis** (outer layer) and the **dermis** (inner layer). Each consists of multiple layers that fulfill various functions. The outside of the epidermis is made up of scales (dead skin cells). It is covered by a protective film produced by the **sebaceous glands**. This film is a natural chemical barrier that serves to hinder the proliferation of viruses, bacteria, fungi, and mold. At the same time, the oil produced by the sebaceous glands keeps the skin flexible and helps repel water. The thick, elastic, dermis, contains the **hair follicles**, **erector muscles** (which make the hair stand up straight), **blood vessels**, sebaceous glands, sweat glands (which are only found in the dermal layer of the footpad), and **nerve endings**. The latter react to external stimuli such as pressure, temperature, and pain and transmit this information to the brain. When a dog's skin is healthy, it usually regenerates very quickly. However, the older a dog is, the longer it will take for its skin to repair itself.

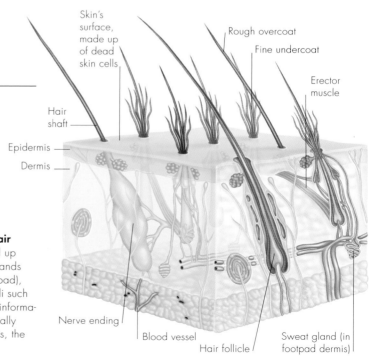

Skin's surface, made up of dead skin cells

Rough overcoat

Fine undercoat

Erector muscle

Hair shaft

Epidermis

Dermis

Nerve ending

Blood vessel

Hair follicle

Sweat gland (in footpad dermis)

BRUSHING AND COMBING

Dogs with a great deal of hair, such as poodles, will of course require more brushing and combing than dogs with smooth coats, such as Boxers. All senior dogs, even shorthaired ones, should be given a quick daily brush in order to stimulate their skin. How often a longhaired dog needs brushing and combing depends on the type of coat it has, but it should be done thoroughly at least once a week (see p121).

In spring and fall, dogs' coats adjust to changing climate conditions by thinning out (spring) or becoming heavier (fall). Today, however, many dogs live in apartments that are kept at relatively constant temperatures. For this reason, many grow their heavier coats much later in the fall. In senior dogs, hormonal disturbances can also lead to difficulties when their coats change. They will then need more grooming so that dead hair is removed quickly, and to ensure it does not end up all over the house.

Use a soft brush to groom a senior dog, one with soft bristles or rubber-tipped metal pins. These brush types are best because they do not irritate or scratch the elderly dog's sensitive skin, and make grooming more enjoyable for it. When grooming longhaired dogs, make sure you get at the undercoat when brushing, not just the overcoat. The easiest way to do this is to part the hair into sections, and brush one section before moving on to the next. Dogs that have silky, luxurious, coats, such as Yorkshire Terriers, do not have protective downy undercoats. More care is needed when you are grooming these types of dogs in order not to damage or irritate their skins.

In longhaired breeds, hair mats up easily under the armpits, around the ears and on the inside legs. You can use a stripping knife to separate the clumps of hair. Despite its name, this instrument does not have a cutting edge. To use it on matted hair, grasp the hair between your thumb and the knife, pull it apart and then thoroughly brush it out. Dogs usually prefer having the knots cut out, however.

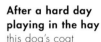

Q WHAT ARE THE MOST FREQUENT CHANGES TO SKIN AND COAT?

A As a dog ages, its muzzle grays, its coat thins, and individual hairs become finer. Due to hormonal changes, dogs that have long, fine coats can develop a thick, lush coat. Other elderly dogs lose hair and can develop bald spots in patches. The skin loses its elasticity, often becomes thicker, and can become dry or oily. Overweight dogs, especially, can develop calluses. Most senior dogs get warts and oil gland tumors (sebaceous adenomas, or cysts) (see p114).

After a hard day playing in the hay this dog's coat needs a good brushing so that it does not mat up.

GROOMING EQUIPMENT

In dog grooming, there is a piece of equipment for every kind of coat

Comb

Two-sided brush

Stripping knife

Brush with soft bristles

Two-sided comb

Rubber brush

CLIPPING AND TRIMMING

Many dog breeds have coats requiring routine clipping or trimming. Senior dogs often have thin coats—sometimes you can even see through to the skin below. When such dogs are clipped, leave at least one-third to two-thirds of an inch (one to two centimeters) of hair. There should be enough hair left to give them adequate protection against the cold and from ultraviolet rays (*see p114*).

During trimming, dead hairs are plucked from a dog's coat using fingers or a stripping knife. This procedure does not hurt the dog in the least and is tolerated patiently by it. Sometimes, however, changes to its skin can make trimming unpleasant for an elderly dog. If this is the case, and if you think your dog would stand for it, you might want to consider clipping its coat on a regular basis instead. Keep in mind that by clipping your dog more frequently, its coat might become finer. Take your dog to a dog-grooming salon for an assessment.

No matter what the breed, aged dogs benefit from routine professional grooming. For example, senior dogs with long or thick coats can find it hard to regulate their body temperatures when it is hot outside, or when they are exercising. When the burden of their coats is removed they often spring to life, even when their coats just have been thinned out, not cut. Although both services are available in dog salons, they are being offered more often in the home as well. And, given a bit of practice, you can also cut and trim your dog's coat by yourself.

A clip or a trim?
It is often best to clip a senior dog's coat rather than to trim it.

Using your fingers, pluck out the dead hair.

With a stripping knife,
dead hair can be quickly and easily.plucked out of a dog's coat.

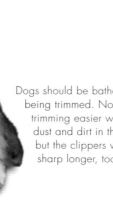

Dogs should be bathed before being trimmed. Not only is trimming easier without dust and dirt in the coat, but the clippers will stay sharp longer, too.

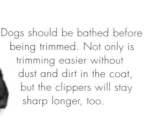

Thinning scissors let you thin out a dog's coat unnoticeably.

BATHING

Most dogs would vote for this too: the rule when bathing dogs is to do so as seldom as possible, but as often as necessary. Always use a special, mild dog shampoo and dilute it with water (about 1 part shampoo to 5 parts water). Place a nonslip mat in the bathtub—old dogs, especially, are not all that steady on their feet. Do not let any shampoo—even tearless shampoo— get into your dog's eyes; use a damp washcloth to wash its face. Cover the dog's ear passages with a cloth, or gently wedge some cotton into them, to protect them from the water. Test the water temperature to make sure the water is not too hot. Then, lather up the dog's coat twice, starting from its head and working down to its paws each time. After this, rinse off the shampoo thoroughly until your dog's coat is squeaky clean. Using a thick towel or a hair dryer, dry your dog immediately so that it does not catch cold.

Special medicinal shampoo formulas have been created by veterinarians for dogs with skin or hair problems and are available from them. Your own veterinarian will select the right type of product line for your dog once the diagnosis has been determined.

When you are bathing a dog, make sure that no shampoo gets into its eyes.

SKIN CARE

Old dogs, especially large and heavy ones, can develop calluses. These are formed by constant pressure to its skin when it is lying down. In general, calluses develop in areas such as the elbows, hocks, or breastbone, which are bony and have very little skin tissue covering them. They can also develop in other areas. The affected skin thickens and becomes callused to protect it from the constant pressure. You can help by rubbing moisturizer into the callused area to keep the skin flexible. This will help prevent fine cracks from developing in the calluses that can turn into stubborn infections. Since a common cause of calluses is lying on hard surfaces, such as tiles or concrete, provide your dog with a soft place to sleep so that its limbs are well cushioned (*see* *p39*).

Calluses are not only look terrible to look at, they can develop fine cracks that become infected.

A large, soft basket offers lots of room to cuddle up in and helps prevent calluses from forming.

GO TO THE VETERINARIAN

when the dog has

→ red and irritated skin

→ very scaly skin

→ a very oily coat

→ hair or skin that gives off a strong odor

→ round marks on its skin

→ skin that is encrusted or hardened

→ a swelling or lump on or under the skin

→ eczema, pimples, or other skin changes

→ a wound

→ external parasites, or their eggs or excrement, on its skin and coat

→ patches of hair loss

→ an urge to scratch itself more often than usual

→ a habit of licking certain patches of its skin excessively

→ no feeling on some parts of its body

Most elderly dogs have warts—often on their faces. These are more of a cosmetic than a health problem, and the warts will only need to be removed when they become infected or irritated, especially those around the eyes. Also, in old dogs, small benign tumors can occur in the oil-producing skin glands (sebaceous adenomas, or cysts) and these can crop up all over a dog's body. They are light in color, hairless, soft to the touch, and can be pushed right down into the skin. These only need to be removed when they cause problems. However, if their numbers increase, or you notice changes to them such as bleeding or irritation, take your dog to the veterinarian, who will inspect them and remove them if necessary.

In areas where its coat is thinner a dog's skin is more exposed to UV-rays, and dogs do get sunburned. This is particularly true for light-skinned, senior dogs. If your dog is going to be exposed to full sunshine, apply sunscreen lotion to these sensitive skin areas in order to protect them. Use sunscreen lotion that has a high protective factor (SPF 30).

Warts can grow anywhere, even right beside an eye.

Warts proliferate
as dogs age. They only need to be removed when they become infected or bother the dog.

OTHER ROUTINE CARE

Caring for a senior dog calls for A to Z service, from the tip of its nose to the tip of its tail. So that you do not forget anything, put down your dog's routine care in your weekly calendar.

EYES

Check your dog's eyes daily. The so-called "sleep" that gathers in the corners of its eyes consists, in large part, of dried secretions. These can be quickly and easily removed with your finger. Secretions that are encrusted can be softened and gently removed with a soft cotton ball dipped in warm water. The dried secretions provide fertile ground for bacteria so if you do not remove them daily, eye infections can readily occur.

In fact, old dogs are particularly susceptible to eye infections. A warning signal for this is a yellow or green discharge coming from its eyes. The most common cause for eye infections is dry eye, which—as its name suggests—is caused when the tear gland fails to produce enough fluid and bacteria invade. Untreated dry eye can also lead to conjunctivitis and abscesses.

Another sign of infection is excess tears. Tears flow more copiously when there is an irritant to the eyeball, such as an eyelash or a foreign particle, an ulcer, conjunctivitis, or blocked tear ducts. When the tear ducts are plugged, tears cannot drain properly down the canal at the back of the dog's nose and flow continuously. Blocked tear ducts can be due to heredity. They are often also caused by mucous and inflammation in the tear ducts, or infections. In some breeds, such as Poodles, blocked tear ducts cause a dark brown stain along the inside corner of their eyes. Tear stains can be removed by carefully cleaning the area with a saltwater solution. Under no circumstances use a chamomile solution since this can irritate a dog's eyes.

To help prevent eye infections, using a small scissors with rounded tips, trim away any hair that can get into your dog's eyes, or use a hair elastic or a clip to tie back its bangs. This is not only more pleasant for the dog, it will also be able to see better without a hairy curtain in front of its eyes.

GO TO THE VETERINARIAN

when

→ the dog's eyes are red

→ the conjunctiva redden

→ there is excessive tearing

→ there is a yellow or green discharge from the eyes

→ the dog scratches its eyes often

→ the dog blinks often

→ the dog often squeezes one or both eyes tightly shut

→ the dog looks cross-eyed

→ the dog is suddenly sensitive to light

→ the dog does not like to be touched around the eyes

→ the dog shows behavioral changes—for example, it is easily startled

→ you notice any other change to your dog's eyes

EARS

A senior dog's ears need especially good care and should be checked over twice a week. A little bit of dirt is normal. Remove it using a soft, lint-free, cloth and a special cleaning product that is available from your veterinarian. Only attempt to remove dirt that is easily visible in the outer ear canal. Do not try to clean out bits of dirt—which can include gum, excess wax, or clumps of hair—that are lodged deeper down in the ear passage. You might end up pushing the foreign particles

Make sure, when you are cleaning a dog's ears, that you do not push any dirt into its ears inadvertently.

further down into the ear canal, especially if you are using cotton swabs. The dislodged dirt can cause an ear infection, or acerbate an already-existing problem. You can also clean your dog's ears by using a special dropper to place the cleaning product directly into the ear passage, which then softens the dirt. When your dog shakes its head, the loosened dirt in the ear is shaken out as well. Your veterinarian can tell you whether or not this method will work on your dog. However, your veterinarian should always clean out dirt that is hard to remove.

Longhaired dog breeds, especially, often have dense hair in and on their ears that attract dirt and hinder the free circulation of air in the ears. You can remove excess hair quite easily using rounded tweezers or special forceps. If you are reluctant to do this yourself, have a dog groomer do it.

To prevent it from matting up, give extra attention to hair that is located on or under the ears when you are brushing dogs that have long earflaps or long hair. Very long ear flaps can also prevent good air circulation in the ears. Given that bacteria love to multiply in warm, humid, conditions, dogs with long ear flaps are more prone to ear infections. For some breeds, such as Scottish Terriers, it is often best to use thinning scissors to cut their ear hair, while for longhaired breeds, trimming or plucking out the thick hair found on their ears may be better.

Dog groomer's tip: use forceps to remove hair from your dog's ears. They are available in pet stores and from your veterinarian.

GO TO THE VETERINARIAN

when

→ the dog's ear reddens inside or outside

→ the ear is very dirty

→ there is a discharge from the ears

→ the ears give off a bad odor

→ the dog scratches its ears excessively

→ the dog constantly holds its head to one side

→ the dog often shakes its head

→ the dog does not react when it is touched on the ear

→ you can feel lumps or swellings

→ you notice any other changes to the dog's ears

TEETH

Tooth and mouth pain can make the lives of many senior dogs miserable. It is often caused by inflammation of the gums (gingivitis) and tooth decay caused when tartar (calculus) is allowed to build up. Tartar is hardened, or mineralized, plaque, which is a mucus film that forms on the teeth. Smaller dog breeds, especially, have a great deal of tartar since their teeth are closer together than those of larger dogs, and harder to clean. There are several ways of keeping a dog's teeth clean. The best method is to regularly feed your dog chew treats such as rawhide bones, bully sticks, cow's ears, beef ligaments, dried vegetable strips, as well as hard dog biscuits and dry dog food. This will automatically reduce the amount of plaque and tartar on its teeth. How often you feed your dog such treats depends to a certain extent on its weight. Some dogs should only eat chew treats two times a week, others remain slim and trim even when they snack on such treats daily (*see p103*). If your dog rarely enjoys chew treats, and usually eats moist food, then dangerous plaque can build up more quickly and turn into tartar.

DENTAL CARE IS IMPORTANT

Two sets of teeth in comparison. Both dogs are ten years old. Smaller dogs (*right*) usually require more dental care since they tend to get more tartar.

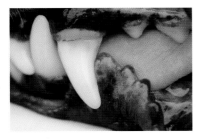

Minimal tartar, healthy gums

Tartar build-up, inflamed gums

To avoid tartar build-up, clean your senior dog's teeth regularly once or twice a week. Special dental hygiene products have been developed for dogs. These are available in pet stores and from the veterinarian. They include dog toothpaste, finger toothbrushes, and mouth rinses. A quick way of cleaning your dog's teeth between regular brushing is by wrapping a damp piece of gauze or toweling around your finger and rubbing it back and forth against your dog's teeth. Make sure you also clean its back teeth. Use regular dental hygiene as an opportunity to inspect your dog's mouth for any

GO TO THE VETERINARIAN

when

→ the dog's gums are red. Healthy gums are pink-colored, and sometimes, depending on the coat, pigmented

→ swellings or lumps appear on the gums

→ the dog often scratches its muzzle

→ you see oozing spots on the gums or mucus membranes

→ your dog has bad breath

→ you can see tartar

→ there are foreign particles in the dog's mouth

→ a tooth is damaged

→ the dog has no sensation in and around its mouth

→ the dog salivates strongly

→ you notice changes to the dog's gums and/or teeth

→ your dog has difficulties eating

→ your dog refuses its food

→ you notice other changes, such as to its bite or to its gums

A toothbrush that can be mounted on a finger.

Dog dental care tools

Rubber tips that massage the dog's gums.

Not all dogs like having their teeth cleaned. To accustom your dog to brushing, be very gentle and praise it frequently during the procedure.

Ice crystals and road salt damage a dog's paws. Rubbing a gel such as petroleum jelly into the paws helps protect them.

Trim long hairs that grow between the dog's pads

changes. Tumors can grow on a dog's gums and inside its mouth (*see p146*). In older dogs, cauliflower-shaped tumors can crop up on the gums, but these are seldom cancerous. However, the latest studies show that they should be removed as soon as possible before they can grow larger and affect the entire mouth.

Only a veterinarian should remove tartar that has built up, since special equipment is required, such as an ultrasonic scaler. After removing the tartar, the veterinarian will thoroughly polish your dog's teeth. This treatment is usually carried out under general anesthesia, which can be very hard on old dogs (*see p148*), so it is best to combine dental care with other, necessary, treatments. However, do not save up too many problems for treatment under general anesthesia solely for this reason, since then your dog would have to be anesthetized for a much longer time.

Since tooth infections are very painful and can lead to your dog refusing its food, do not wait until its gums and teeth have been infected before having tartar removed. Even worse, a persistent gum disease may cause toxins and bacteria to spread into a dog's internal organs, such as the heart, kidneys, and liver, and damage them. This is also why a tooth that is badly infected should be removed without delay by the veterinarian.

PAWS AND NAILS

If your dog is limping or favoring a paw, inspect its footpad thoroughly for cuts and punctures or foreign particles. Even small injuries can lead to infection and inflammation because the dog often licks them obsessively, irritating them. If you discover foreign particles, such as thorns, splinters, or glass shards in a paw, remove them yourself if you can with tweezers or forceps and keep an eye on the wound. Deep punctures can often become infected. If you cannot remove the foreign particle yourself, have the veterinarian do it.

Longhaired dogs, especially, grow thick, long, hair between their footpads, even more so when they are older. Trim this hair back as much as you can using rounded scissors. This will prevent soil and snow from clumping up underneath the footpad, which can hurt your dog when it walks.

Senior dogs often suffer from brittle, cracked footpad. To help counteract this, rub a special moisturizer, cream, or petroleum jelly onto them. In winter, regular application of such lotions will help also protect your dog's paws from road salt damage to its footpad.

When dogs are walked primarily on hard surfaces, such as concrete, their toenails usually do not need very much trimming at all since concrete naturally abrades the nails. But generally old dogs are walked less often than younger ones. And too, they are usually walked on soft springy surfaces to protect their joints (*see p24*). For these reasons, senior dogs' toenails need clipping more often. It is high time for a pedicure when your dog's toenails are so long that they start to curve in or in some way affect the dog's gait. Pay special attention to the upper back toenail—the dewclaw. Since this nail never touches the ground, it does not wear down naturally, and can snag on textiles, for example, if it is not trimmed.

GO TO THE VETERINARIAN

when

→ you find foreign particles in a paw

→ a paw is injured

→ a nail is torn off in whole or in part

→ a nail is split or very brittle

→ you can feel swellings or lumps in a paw

→ the paw is red and inflamed, or you can see pus

→ the dog licks one of its paws excessively

→ a paw gives off a bad odor

→ a spot on the dog's paw weeps

→ your dog has no sense of touch on one of its paws

→ the dog does not want to put its weight on one of its paws

→ you notice other changes to a paw

Being well prepared
allows a senior dog to have more fun frolicking in the snow.

Do not reach for a human manicure set to trim your dog's nails. A specially designed toenail clipper should be used. These are available from the pet store. Have your veterinarian or dog groomer show you how to cut your dog's nails in the right way. Do not cut off too much nail all at once, otherwise you might injure the blood vessel under the nail. If your dog's nails are light in color, you often will be able to see a pinkish color where the vein lies. If your dog has black nails, hold up its nail against a strong light to see the vein. Should you inadvertently cut into the nail blood vessel, you can stop the bleeding by rubbing a piece of laundry soap over the wound, or firmly applying a sterile pressure bandage to it.

"Many dog owners have had good results using homeopathic medicines..."

Old dogs' toenails are often brittle, and break and split easily. Many dog owners have had good results using homeopathic medicines and food

Trimming a dog's nails is easy with a good nail clipper.

Long nails affect the way a dog walks, break easily, and split often.

Cut the toenail at the same angle to which it has worn down through natural abrasion

supplements (*see p104*). If you would like to try out these preparations, ask your animal homeopath or your veterinarian for some recommendations.

ANAL CARE

When defecating, dogs with long coats often dirty the hair in their anal region, especially when they have diarrhea. This can lead to irritation, inflammations, and infections, and also is a hygiene problem. The best way to prevent this problem is by trimming short the hair around the anus so that it can be cleaned quickly and easily. You can treat mild irritations to the anus yourself with a healing ointment from the pharmacy.

CHECKING THE ANAL SACS

The anal sacs are located below and to each side of a dog's anal opening. They produce a scented fluid that is expelled onto the dog's stool when it defecates. This scent plays an important role in dog communication. Excess fluid usually flows back into the dog's rectum.

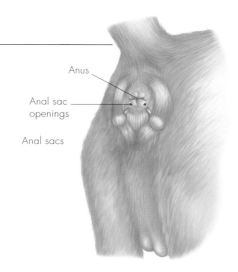

Anus

Anal sac openings

Anal sacs

Anal sacs

Heredity, soft stool, or diarrhea can lead to a blockage of the anal sacs. Senior dogs often suffer from this problem. If your dog starts to scoot its rear end along the ground, licks its anus often, or jumps up suddenly when it lies down or is already lying down, these are clear signs of a blockage and fluid accumulation. When the fluid that has built up in the anal sacs is not emptied out, infections or even abscesses can result. It is best if the veterinarian does this although you can do it yourself with practice. There are two main reasons for this: injuries can occur if the procedure is not done correctly, and, if the veterinarian diagnoses an infection and the sacs need draining, antibiotics can be given to your dog immediately to help prevent further infection and speed up the healing process.

Elderly male dogs that have not been neutered more readily get benign tumors on their anuses (perianal adenomas or tumors). For this reason, check your dog for signs of swellings or lumps in the anal region during your weekly inspection. Any you discover will need to be removed; otherwise, your dog will have problems defecating. Treatment to prevent further perianal tumors usually includes neutering the dog since a primary cause of their growth is the presence of the male hormone testosterone.

GO TO THE VETERINARIAN

when

→ the dog's anus gives off a very strong odor

→ the dog licks its anus frequently

→ the dog scoots along the ground

→ you can see or feel swellings or lumps in the anal area

→ the anus looks red and irritated

→ there is infectious pus on the anus

→ the dog is no longer sensitive to touch in the anal area

→ you notice any other changes to the anal area

ROUTINE CARE SCHEDULE FOR YOUR SENIOR DOG

Daily	→ a quick brush and/or comb → check the eyes and paws, clean if needed
Two to three times a week	→ check its ears, clean if needed → check its teeth and gums → clean its teeth
Weekly	→ thoroughly examine skin, hair and all body openings → brush and comb your dog thoroughly
Monthly	→ check its toenails, trim if needed
As needed	→ bath → trim → clip

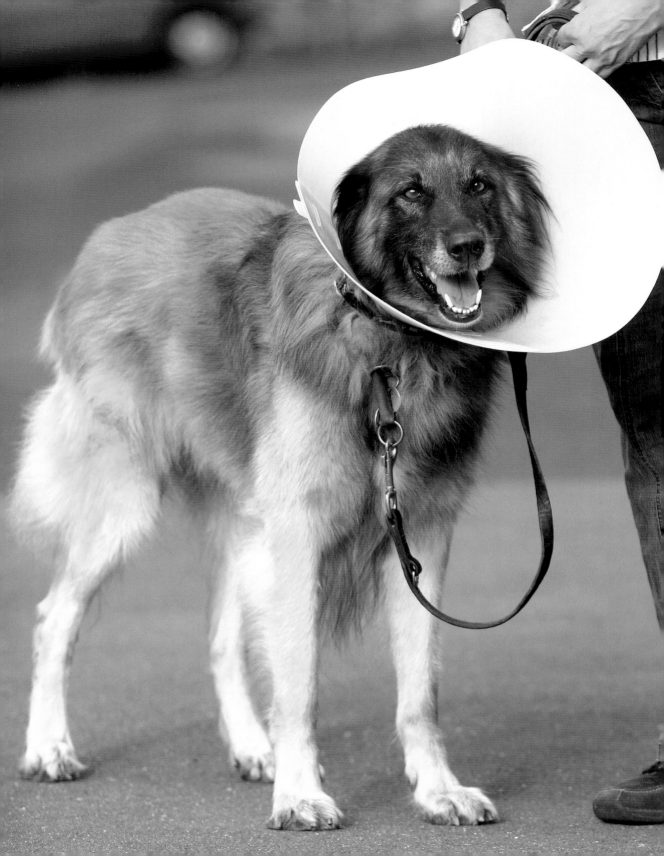

HEALTH IN OLD AGE

IN LOVE WITH LIFE, SPRIGHTLY, and healthy: this is how we would like our dogs to be when they are old. However, just as in humans, large and small aches and pains, and sometimes, of course, diseases can arise with age. You can do much to prevent many illnesses by feeding your dog the right diet and keeping it under ideal conditions. Still, despite the most loving care, illnesses can occur.

The better you know your dog, the more quickly you will be able to detect changes to its usual pattern of behavior and its physical capabilities that might be a reason for concern. Observe your canine senior carefully so that you can report these changes to the veterinarian, who will then investigate any suspected signs of illness and come up with a diagnosis. The earlier an illness is detected, the better the chances of curing it or easing the symptoms.

Working hand in hand with your veterinarian, you can also contribute a great deal to your dog's recovery by giving it the loving care and attention it needs. Unfortunately, not every disease is curable. When a dog has an incurable disease, the goal has to be to preserve the dog's quality of life. With the right care and attention, and the proper medicines, many chronically ill dogs reach a ripe old age and remain physically fit for a long time. Your veterinarian will be your confidant and advisor and a steadfast support.

ROUTINE EXAMINATIONS
and prevention

"Give me a high-five"
If your dog can give its paw on command or even lie down on its side or stomach, for example, a regular checkup can turn into an amusing practice session.

When you are carrying out routine dog care at home, you will notice changes that might signify ill health. But regular examinations by the veterinarian, and proper preventive care, are part of disease prevention.

HOME EXAMINATION

Once a week you should take the time to thoroughly examine your senior canine housemate (*see p121*) and feel along its entire body. Check its joints: do they seem hot or swollen? Is your dog insensitive to touch in certain spots, or do you notice other changes that might necessitate a visit to the veterinarian (*see pp110–14*)? In addition to these checks, weigh your dog every two weeks (*see pp105–07*). If your dog has lost or gained weight radically you need to try to discover the reason why with the help of your veterinarian. Take a good look at your dog's stool, too. Changes to its consistency, color, and frequency provide important health indicators (*see p134*).

EXAMINATION BY THE VETERINARIAN

Large dogs six years and older, and small dogs eight years and older, should be taken to the veterinarian twice yearly for thorough routine checkups. The veterinarian will examine the dog's heart and lungs, assess its diet, check its muscles and coordination, palpitate its abdomen, flex its joints, evaluate the color of and deposits on its gums, take its temperature, and check its eyes, ears, teeth and mouth, paws and nails, anal region, genitals, spine, and skin and coat for any sign of abnormalities.

Since, in their early stages, many illnesses cannot be detected by external examination alone, blood and urine samples should also be taken during a routine examination. Even when your dog is in excellent health now, down the road these test results can provide important comparative data. They can help in the diagnosis and eventual treatment of problems and illnesses that can occur.

If the veterinarian discovers some sort of abnormality during a routine checkup, further tests can be carried out on the spot to get to the root of the problem.

VACCINATIONS

Routine vaccinations prevent many serious diseases—some of which are deadly. For this reason, after your dog has had its course of essential vaccinations, we recommend that you keep up its immunization against canine distemper, infectious canine hepatitis, canine parvovirus, leptospiros and rabies.

Depending on the risks that your dog is exposed to, other regular vaccinations might be advisable. These include vaccinations against diseases such as kennel cough (which can be contracted by frequent contact with many dogs) or Lyme disease (which is carried by ticks). Evaluate your dog's vaccination needs with your veterinarian.

"Once a week, you should take the time to thoroughly examine your senior canine housemate and feel along its entire body."

There is a great deal of discussion as to whether or not old dogs need the full vaccination program or if it is enough to refresh their immunization with booster shots at infrequent intervals. Of course, you might like to save your dog from being vaccinated unnecessarily. Just keep in mind that at any time your dog can come into contact with an infected dog, such as a stray, and become ill itself or pass on the infection to other dogs. Proof of vaccination against rabies is generally required for dogs that are traveling with you into other jurisdictions or taking part in dog shows. Since rabies vaccination requirements vary from one jurisdiction to another, and can change when there is a rabies outbreak, check with your veterinarian to find out the latest requirements before you travel. Also, ask your veterinarian for advice about which vaccinations and booster shots your dog should have, and when.

WORMING

There are many different recommendations as to how often a dog should be wormed—twice or three times a year as a matter of routine, or only when it has been infected. If children are living in the house, or your dog often eats a mouse, carrion, or the excrement of other animals during walks, you probably should worm it frequently. This also makes it less likely that your dog will pass on worms to humans, who can also be infected by tapeworms, roundworms and hookworms. However, if a dog is already suffering from a chronic disease of the internal organs, the drugs used to worm it can be hard on its system. In such cases, it is best to have the veterinarian first test the dog's stool for worms and then only treat the dog for them if they are present. Switch the drugs you use now and then since not every drug works against every type of worm, and worms can also build up a resistance to the active ingredients in drugs.

Even dogs that are well cared for can be infected with worms. All it takes is for your canine friend to eat carrion or animal excrement that it finds along the way.

If you dog scratches constantly, the cause could be fleas. Dark "flea dirt" in its fur and on its skin is a sign your dog has fleas.

Preparations for application on the neck

EXTERNAL PARASITES

Parasites can infect dogs with diseases such as Lyme disease, meningitis, (FSME) and babesia. Fleas can infect dogs with tapeworms, and the saliva in fleabites gives some dogs skin allergies, causing them to scratch and bite the wounds. Mites and lice often cause skin problems, too.

Either as a preventive measure or during an infestation, you can protect your dog from parasites by using an insecticide provided by your veterinarian. These usually come in the form of preparations that are applied to the dog's skin around its neck, or insecticidal shampoos. If the dog is suffering from a parasite infestation, its home environment also has to be treated. Preparations are sold that treat the infestation on the dog and also kill the flea larvae and nits found in its living environment.

If a tick has attached itself to your dog, quickly remove it with special tweezers or forceps and apply an antibacterial cream to the spot. Do not use your fingers. Make sure you do not squeeze the tick when removing it, this can cause it to release its saliva into the dog's bloodstream. A tick's saliva can carry toxins and disease. Do not dribble oil, alcohol, or other liquids onto the parasite since this too might lead to its releasing saliva.

YOU & YOUR VETERINARIAN

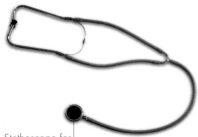

Stethoscope for listening to the dog's heart and lungs.

Your dog's health lies in your hands and in the hands of its veterinarian. Trust and excellent communication are crucial to the optimal care of your senior dog.

The veterinarian is an important advisor who often shares a wide range of emotions with dog owners such as joy after successful treatment, sadness when a negative diagnosis is made, worry in times of crisis, or the sadness of saying farewell to a beloved canine companion.

TRUSTING YOUR VETERINARIAN

It is extremely important that you trust your veterinarian both as a person and as a medical authority. The veterinarian should take you and your concerns seriously, have time for you, explain diagnoses and treatments so that you can understand them, and deal with your dog in a professional and caring way. The veterinarian is your contact for routine examinations and the first person you turn to when problems arise. In order to be able to help your dog quickly in an emergency, the animal practice should located fairly close to your home. Your veterinarian, or substitute, should also be available on weekends and, ideally, should be willing to make emergency house calls. The practice should be equipped with X-ray and ultrasound machines for making diagnoses, and a laboratory for preliminary testing of blood and urine. If these samples need to be evaluated by an outside laboratory, then the test results should be available the following week. The veterinarian should be able to carry out routine surgery in the practice, and there should always be a second trained assistant present to watch over the anesthetized dog and assist during surgery.

If the practice does not have the right equipment to make a diagnosis or treat your dog, or if a second opinion is needed, then your veterinarian should not hesitate to refer you to a specialized veterinarian. This can be to a specialist in small animal medicine with an emphasis on dermatology, surgery, cardiology, internal medicine, or eye disease, for example, or an animal clinic that covers these and other specialties.

THE SELF-CONFIDENT DOG OWNER

Ask your veterinarian to explain all diagnoses and their treatments, including holistic treatment, and all prescribed medicines. Ask if there is something you do not understand. If it sometimes happens that you are very nervous during a visit to the veterinarian, and only recall important points you wanted to raise when you are back home again, note down any important questions ahead of time. And do not hesitate to get a second opinion if you are uncertain about the diagnosis or therapy.

Dental care under anesthetic is a routine procedure carried out on senior dogs in small animal veterinary practices.

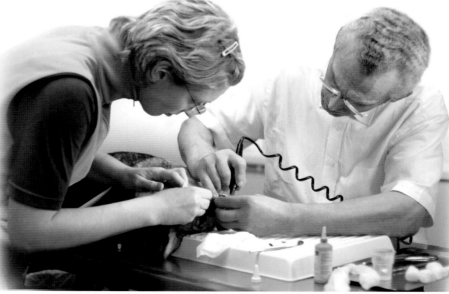

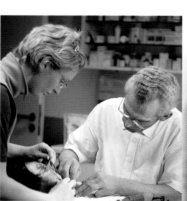

A second veterinarian or trained veterinary assistant should always be on hand to monitor the anesthetic and assist during surgery.

It is an ideal situation,
when you deal with the same person in an animal clinic each time, a veterinarian that your dog will come to know and trust over the course of time.

SHOULD I VISIT MY DOG IN THE CLINIC?

It really depends on you and your dog whether visits are a good idea or not. If your dog copes well with being left alone again after you leave, if you motivate it positively instead of passing on your own worries, and if the veterinarian has no objections, there is no reason not to visit your dog. However, you should show understanding when visits to a very sick dog are frowned upon or even forbidden in the first few days after your dog has been admitted. It is more important that the dog is properly examined and gets enough rest, and that its condition is stabilized.

In an animal hospital,
the tools and equipment are usually state-of-the art and the personnel is well trained. Serious diseases are diagnosed and treated here.

THE ANIMAL HOSPITAL

Animal hospitals are usually staffed with specialized veterinarians, offer round-the-clock service, and are well equipped with sophisticated diagnostic tools and equipment. These include endoscopes (investigative instruments that are introduced into the dog's body); electrocardiograms (ECGs), which chart heart rhythm; X-ray machines; and ultrasound scanners. Some animal hospitals also have CT scanners, a kind of X-ray machine that reveals the soft tissues. Laboratories in these animal hospitals have all the apparatus they need to test blood, urine, and stool immediately. During surgery, anesthetics can be administered through a breathing mask. Since dosages can be individually adjusted during surgery, and the canine patients are carefully monitored the entire time they are anesthetized, this is a particularly gentle method (see p148).

Just as in a human hospital, and depending on its specialty, an animal hospital can carry out every type of treatment, such as chemotherapy. It can also perform most types of complicated surgery, such as birthing help, joint surgery, spinal surgery, and implanting heart pacemakers.

Dogs are kept overnight in animal hospitals for various reasons. They might be under observation, in intensive or postoperative care, or be cared for because a dog owner is not in a position to nurse his or her dog. The canine patients are housed in a special room, and cared for, treated, and monitored around-the-clock by professionals. A veterinarian is always available in case of emergency. This type of care is not cheap, however. Expert personnel and the latest technical equipment have their price.

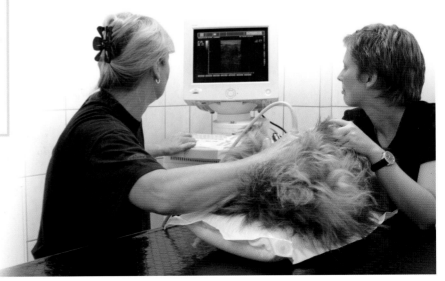

THE RIGHT KIND OF HELP

Following your veterinarian's instructions to the letter is the best way you can support the treatment of your acutely or chronically ill dog. This means you will be, in fact, a partner in therapy.

CONSULTING THE VETERINARIAN

When your dog is ill, ask your veterinarian whether or not the animal needs a great deal of rest, what kind and amount of exercise is recommended, if it should avoid excitement (for example, visits and excursions) and whether or not it is allowed to be in contact with other dogs.

If your dog is not allowed to move around very much (after surgery, for example), it is best kept in a dog crate, one in which it can stand upright, turn around easily, and stretch out comfortably. Make sure to line the bottom of the crate with a soft mat or thick blanket to protect the dog from the cold floor, and that the dog has enough fresh drinking water within reach.

ADMINISTERING MEDICINE

Many senior dogs need to be given medicine daily. If this is the case, then follow the instructions provided by your veterinarian. Some medicines have to be given before or with meals and at specific intervals. Never stop administering prescribed medicine abruptly without first consulting your veterinarian, even when your dog's health seems to be much improved. Doing this can cause a relapse, or the dog might build up a resistance to a drug such as an antibiotic. On a piece of paper, write down when and how often medicine should be administered and put it where you will see it—in the medicine cabinet.

Giving a pill

In the pharmacy or at your veterinarian's, you can purchase a pill sorter. This is a plastic box with compartments for each day of the week. You can fill it up ahead of time with the pills your dog needs daily during the coming week so that you do not forget any.

A plastic covering keeps this dog's bandage dry and clean. The covering should be removed at home.

THE RIGHT TEMPERATURE

A dog's normal body temperature usually ranges between 100.5°F and 102.5°F (38.1–39.2°C), although larger and older dogs usually measure at the lower end of the scale. To find out a dog's temperature, first lubricate the tip of a fever thermometer with petroleum jelly. Use a digital thermometer since older types made of glass can break too easily when a dog decides to resist. Hold the dog's tail up high, and insert the thermometer into the dog's rectum at a slight angle so that it touches the mucous membranes. Keep the hand that holds the thermometer in contact with the dog to keep track of its movements and lessen the danger of injuring it. If the dog's temperature is under 99.7°F (37.6°C), or over 103°F (39.4°C), you should take it to the veterinarian for examination.

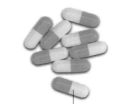

When giving a dog pills, make sure to adhere to the schedule

The results are displayed digitally

WHEN A DOG DECIDES TO BE DIFFICULT

Many dogs really dislike having drops or ointment put in their eyes or ears and try to pull away. If this is the case with your dog, then you will need to have someone help you hold the dog in place to minimize injury to it. To protect yourself, you might also have to muzzle your dog if it strongly resists treatment.

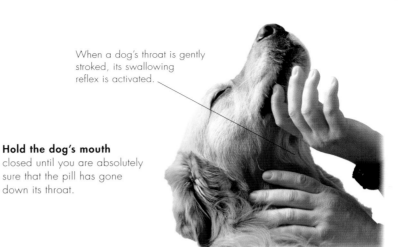

When a dog's throat is gently stroked, its swallowing reflex is activated.

Hold the dog's mouth closed until you are absolutely sure that the pill has gone down its throat.

Q CAN I ADMINISTER HUMAN MEDICINES TO MY DOG?

A There are, in fact, many kinds of medicines made for humans that can also be used for dogs. However, always leave the decision up to a veterinarian! First of all, a diagnosis should be made before any drugs are given, second, the active ingredients in drugs for humans can provoke different reactions in dogs—sometimes they are undesirable, even dangerous, ones. Our conclusion: do not experiment!

Q DO DOGS KNOW WHEN THEY HAVE REACHED THEIR LIMITS?

A Many dogs know their own limits. However, some do not and need careful monitoring so that they do not do too much or do not perform certain kinds of movements. This is especially true when a dog suffers from a muscle, bone, or joint disorder.

Some sorters have enough compartments for several weeks and are ideal for a longer trip away. There are many ways to give a dog a pill:

- If your dog tends to be greedy, mix its medicine into its food. Usually, it will gobble up the medicine along with the food.
- Today, more and more pharmaceutical companies are producing pills for dogs that are designed to taste good, including analgesics and worming pills. Most dogs happily will eat them out of your hand as though they were treats. Ask your veterinarian if the medicine your dog needs is also available in treat form.
- Open your dog's mouth and push the pill over the hump of its tongue and as far back into its mouth as possible. Then, holding the dog's mouth closed, stroke its chin and throat, which will activate the swallowing reflex. Some dogs will resist, which can be stressful for both of you. You can also buy a pill dispenser from your veterinarian or pet shop—this will make giving your dog a pill easier.
- Hide pills in tasty food your dog relishes such as small pieces of bacon or cheese. A finicky dog can, perhaps, be tricked if you first feed it a piece of cheese without a pill inside, followed by a piece containing a pill. The dog will usually eat the second piece without first checking it over. Or, you can dangle the next treat in front of its nose—usually, it will gulp it down in a hurry. Some veterinarians use a pill-coater to coat pills with tastes appealing to dogs. This also simplifies administering pills.
- You can also dissolve the pills in water, fill a plastic syringe with the solution, and spray it directly into the dog's mouth. Insert the syringe at the side of its mouth, between its teeth, and try to squirt the liquid as far back into its mouth as possible.

Giving drops

As with pills, you can also make giving your dog drops a more pleasant experience by hiding them in tasty bits of food. If this is not prudent—if your dog is on a strict diet for example—or possible, use a pipette or plastic syringe to introduce the liquid medicine into the side of its mouth. When just one or two drops are all that is needed, it is usually enough to dribble them onto the dog's nose. The dog will then lick them off. If the dog is still not cooperating, you can also try thinning out the drops with water or cold beef bouillon to make them taste better to the dog.

Administering eyedrops and eye ointment

To give your dog eyedrops, gently pull apart the dog's upper and lower eyelids using your thumb and index finger. Then squeeze the eyedrops onto the eye and release the eyelids. It is very important to avoid touching any part of the eye with the tip of the applicator since this can result in bacteria entering the eye. Also, the remaining eyedrops can become contaminated and cause an eye infection. Single doses are more hygienic than bottles.

When applying eye ointment, start off in the same way as above. So as not to dirty the applicator, you can put ointment on your finger, for example, and then carefully apply the ointment to the inside lower eyelid. Be very careful not to touch the surface of the eye!

Q **WHAT SHOULD I DO WHEN I FIND A PILL LYING AROUND ON THE CARPET?**

A Some dogs are talented magicians! They pretend they swallowed the pills you gave them and then, later on, discretely let them drop from their mouths. If you find pills up to about two hours after you gave your dog the last dose, and you are **absolutely** sure that these are the same pills, then you can give the dog these, or new ones, again. If you are uncertain, it is better to **do nothing**. Rather, wait until it is time to give your dog its next pills and just administer the usual amount. Otherwise, you run the risk of giving it an overdose, which is worse than a missed dose.

Insert the syringe at the side of the dog's mouth.

Carefully pull apart the dog's eyelids.

When administering medicine it is important to be careful but also to show confidence. If you hesitate, your dog will pick up on this and become uncertain, too. As a reward, give the dog a nice treat afterward.

EARLY TRAINING

Practice administering medicine to your dog when it is healthy. A treat given as a reward motivates most canines enormously, and your dog will associate something positive with taking medicine. During "pill training," use tasty morsels of food instead of pills. Artificial tears can serve as real eye drops, and ear wash solutions as real eardrops.

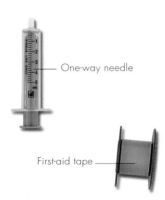

One-way needle

First-aid tape

Administering eardrops and ear ointment

Warm the bottle of eardrops between your hands before you put the drops in your dog's ear so that the liquid will not be too cold. Hold the dog's head still and pull its earflap slightly up and back so that you can see the inside of its ear. Insert the tip of the applicator or tube into the ear canal only as far as is recommended on the instruction sheet that comes with the medicine. Most eardrop medication bottles come with an insertion guide. Squeeze the bottle until the correct dosage has been administered, remove it, put the earflap back in place, and give your canine patient a reward.

Applying ointment

Depending on the type of ointment that has been prescribed, you might need to wear disposable gloves to protect your hands. Unless the dog has an open wound or eczema, thoroughly rub the ointment into the dog's skin so that it reaches the right spot and does not just stay on the coat's surface.

The most difficult part about treating a dog with ointment is not in its application, but rather in preventing the dog from licking it off. You might have to put an Elizabethan collar on it (*see p149*) so that it cannot reach the treated spot. By putting children's socks or special dog shoes over the dog's hind paws, you can prevent the dog from scratching the affected area. As an alternative, you can cover the area with a piece of light children's clothing, cotton stocking, or a special garment purchased from the veterinarian or at the pet store. Taking your dog for a walk will also help distract it.

THE SENIOR DOG'S FIRST-AID KIT

- → Disposable gloves
- → Round-tipped scissors and tweezers
- → Plastic syringes
- → Digital thermometer
- → Emergency blanket
- → Burn-relief gel-pack
- → Antibiotic first-aid ointment
- → Tick tweezers
- → Antidiarrhea pills
- → Light analgesics

- → Eyewash drops
- → Fructose cubes
- → Assorted bandages
- → Gauze roll and pads
- → Triangular sling
- → Pressure bandages
- → Absorbent cotton balls
- → First-aid tape
- → Muzzle and leash
- → Wound disinfectant

A roll of bandages

Your dog's personal pharmacy
Since each senior dog is different, discuss the best items to keep in your senior dog's medicine cabinet with your veterinarian. You might need to add some extra medicines or special equipment to the standard stock. Regularly check the expiry dates of all stocked medicines—from pills to eardrops—and replace them before they have expired.

NATURAL HEALING METHODS

There are many natural, or holistic, healing methods that activate the body's immune system and support the healing process. Some of these methods are: acupuncture to combat pain, degenerative diseases of the skeletal, joint and muscle system, and various diseases of the internal organs and metabolism; homeopathic medicines to fight various conditions such using flower essences (Bach flowers) to treat behavioral problems (i.e. fear and uncertainty); and magnetic therapy to help dogs with musculoskeletal system injuries and diseases. Some methods are commonly accepted therapies such as physical therapy and acupuncture, and many herbal medicines; some do not have a scientific seal of approval but numerous dog owners and veterinarians report astonishing results from them, as do we.

Purple coneflower *(Echinacea purpurea)* strengthens the immune system.

Acupuncture needles in the dog's skin

Acupuncture
Energy flows through the body along lines of energy (meridian lines). Placing needles at specific points along these lines is supposed to free blockages in the energy flow.

Professional treatment

Natural healing methods do not make veterinary practices superfluous, but are to be seen as complementary therapies. Before complementary or alternative treatment is started, the first step is always to consult with your veterinarian who then will make a diagnosis and design a treatment plan. Even though some healing therapies are considered very gentle, this does not mean that they can be used for all conditions and without taking previous illnesses into account. Nor does it mean these therapies are free from side effects—allergic reactions might occur, for example. They can, in fact, intensify some illnesses or even trigger them. For this reason, always turn to a trained natural healing professional who will either perform the therapy or supervise its application. Depending on the type of therapy your dog needs, you may consult a specialized veterinarian, veterinary massage therapist, veterinary homeopath, or holistic veterinary medicine practitioner. This is why we have not provided any instructions; every treatment must be individually tailored to a dog according to the diagnosis that has been made for it.

Magnetic therapy
is often used to combat spinal disorders. It is supposed to promote healing, and reduce pain through the use of a magnetic field.

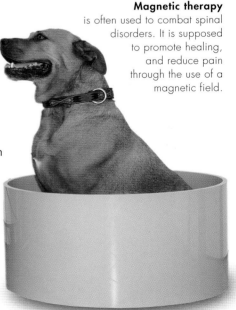

THE RIGHT STEPS TO TAKE

SYMPTOMS	GO TO THE VETERINARIAN….
Breathing is shallow, labored, very fast or slow	Right away if the dog has trouble breathing (see p136)
Lethargy	Right away
Diarrhea (frequent, watery or blood is present in the stool)	Right away
Vomiting (frequent, very colored or the vomit contains blood)	Right away
Retching without vomiting	Right away
Very sweet breath	Right away
Yellow-colored eyes or mucous membranes	Right away
The tongue turns blue after exercise	Right away
Cramps, hunched-over posture	Right away
Lurching, uncertain movements	Right away
Fever	Right away, when other signs of illness appear, otherwise on the same day
Vaginal discharge	Right away, when other signs of illness appear, otherwise on the same day
Constipation or straining unsuccessfully to defecate	Right away, when other signs of illness appear. On the next day if there is no improvement
Pain (see p146)	On the same day
Sudden, inexplicable, excessive thirst	On the same day
Problems or pain when urinating, blood in urine, no urine, or greatly reduced quantity of urine	On the same day
Lameness or limping, walking on three legs	On the same day
Conspicuous changes in behavior	On the same day
Light diarrhea	Easily digestible food (see p104), then within 24 hours if there is no improvement or other signs of illness appear
Vomiting once or twice	Fasting for eight hours or easily digestible food (see p104), then within 24 hours if there is no improvement or other signs of illness appear
The dog does not drink, refuses its food, becomes exhausted easily	If there is no improvement within 24 hours or other signs of illness appear
Incontinence (see p144)	If there is no improvement within 24 hours or other signs of illness appear
Coughing	If there is no improvement within 24 hours or other signs of illness appear

Physical therapy

Physical therapy is an umbrella term covering many different therapies such as physical rehabilitation, massage, electrotherapy, and thermotherapy (warm and cold treatments).

It is primarily used to treat skeletal, joint, and muscle problems such as arthritis, temporary lameness, lameness or stiffness after surgery, or broken bone, or hip problems. Depending on the problem, the goal is to maintain or improve your senior dog's mobility, build up its endurance, build up its muscles, reduce pain, reduce stress and tension, boost its metabolism, or just simply improve its well-being and relax it.

Stimulating the skin around the jaws

Physical therapy
makes the joints more flexible. Depending on the underlying disease, its goal is to restore mobility to normal or to keep it at the same level.

EMERGENCIES

Suddenly and unexpectedly, an emergency can happen. One day, a very severe—possibly life-threatening—illness or accident might befall your dog. If this occurs, you must take swift, decisive action. Your dog will require immediate veterinary attention.

SHOCK

In a medical emergency, a dog's circulatory system sometimes fails. This is known as shock. The organs and body tissues are no longer supplied with enough blood and therefore are no longer supplied with enough oxygen. This is a life-threatening condition! When your dog is in shock, or even when you are not completely sure but suspect shock, cover it with a blanket and bring it to the veterinarian without even a minute's delay. The dog must be treated immediately!

You can check the blood supply to a dog's body by measuring the amount of time it takes for the capillaries, the body's smallest blood vessels, to fill. To do this, press on the dog's gums with your thumb. There will be a temporary white spot. A healthy dog's gums will return to their normal pink color within seconds; those of a dog in shock will take longer. Other signs of shock are pale mucous membranes, a quick but weak pulse, very shallow breathing, and weakness and lethargy, or even complete collapse. The dog will be cold and might be restless.

BE PREPARED!

Get ready for an emergency by programming all your veterinarian's telephone numbers (cell and office), and the number of the nearest animal hospital, into your own cell and home telephones. Have a muzzle and leash on hand, and make sure there is always a first-aid kit in your car.

Shock can be caused by heavy blood loss after an injury, burns, extreme fear or pain, ingestion of toxic substances, allergic reactions, or heatstroke. Severe internal organ disease such as liver, kidney, or heart disease can also cause shock. If this is the case, dogs will collapse, lose consciousness for a few seconds, vomit, or defecate or urinate uncontrollably. Do not lose any time, consult a veterinarian immediately.

FIRST AID IN AN EMERGENCY

Clear the dog's airways

1 The dog's airways should be kept clear. Gently pull its tongue out of its mouth. Make sure the dog does not choke on its own vomit.

2 A dog has to be given mouth-to-nose respiration if it has stopped breathing. Close the dog's mouth. Blow air into its nostrils for about 3 seconds and then open its mouth briefly. Repeat about 10 to 20 times a minute until the dog starts breathing again.

3 Check 4 times in one minute, to see whether the dog's heart is beating (see above). If you cannot detect a heartbeat, you will have to give it cardiac compressions along with mouth-to-nose respiration.

4 If you cannot feel the dog's pulse, you must give it compressions without delay. Move the dog onto its right side. Place the heel of one hand on the dog's chest over its heart, lay the other on top of the first (see left). Press down at regular intervals in the direction of the dog's throat about 100 times a minute for large dogs, 120 times a minute for small dogs. Try to keep to the following rhythm: 15 seconds of compressoins followed by 10 seconds of mouth-to-nose resuscitation until you can feel the dog's pulse and it starts breathing on its own.

ILLNESS IN OLD AGE

Almost every type of illness can crop up during any phase of a dog's life. Some begin to develop during its prime and only show up later, when the dog is old.

Despite this, there are many illnesses that typically arise in the last phase of a dog's life. It is our intention not only to discuss some of these diseases but, above all, to describe their symptoms, so that—in consultation with a veterinarian—treatment can begin as early as possible. Unfortunately it is not possible to discuss all diseases in detail.

Many diseases of old age are degenerative diseases that are caused by wear and tear to the joints or internal organs (*see p11*). There is no way of healing these kinds of diseases. Treatment focuses instead on maintaining a dog's quality of life, slowing down the disease's progress, and reducing pain. It is especially difficult to choose the kind of therapy, and how much of it, an elderly dog needs. This must be decided on a case-by-case basis. We cannot recommend any particular therapy; our intent is to describe the symptoms of various diseases so that you will be more alert to changes in your dog that signal it has an illness.

Slow but steady improvement
Choosing the best kind of therapy for your dog has to be decided on an individual basis.

MUSCLES, JOINTS, AND BONES

Many senior dogs have problems with their "aging" bones; some suffer more, some less. Spinal disorders or joint disease can turn into emergencies when, suddenly, your canine companion hardly can move, or cannot move at all. Since in old dogs, muscles and sinews no longer give much support to their spines, many of them suffer from slipped disks, which can cause severe pain, stiffness, and lameness.

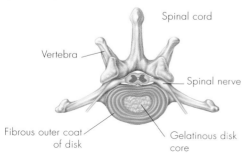

Spinal cord

Vertebra

Spinal nerve

Fibrous outer coat of disk

Gelatinous disk core

A HEALTHY DISK

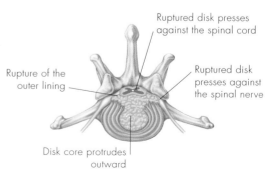

Ruptured disk presses against the spinal cord

Rupture of the outer lining

Ruptured disk presses against the spinal nerve

Disk core protrudes outward

A SLIPPED DISK

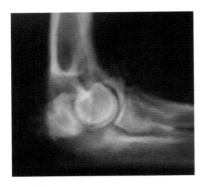

Joint deterioration
Arthrosis can be seen on an X-ray as a thickening of the joint bones.

ARTHRITIS

In contrast to arthrosis, arthritis is an inflammation of the joints. This can cause, be caused by, or accompany arthrosis, which is a degeneration of the cartilage that surrounds aging joints. Dogs of all ages can suffer from arthritis, which, like arthrosis, is a very painful disease. As is the case with arthrosis, arthritis is treated with analgesics and anti-inflammatory medicines.

Arthrosis

Arthrosis is one of the most common illnesses affecting the mobility of senior dogs. It is an incurable degenerative disease that can befall any joint.

In order to protect the ends of the bones in a joint from rubbing against one another, a cartilage layer covers the ends of bones. To allow the bones to move freely, a membrane lining the capsule surrounding the joints secretes a lubricating fluid that nourishes the cartilage and must be replenished continuously. If there is a decrease in the amount of fluid produced, or its composition changes for the worst, then the previously tough and flexible cartilage starts deteriorating. Then, if the bones in the joint start to splinter as a result, the protective cartilage deteriorates even more rapidly and becomes inflamed. This leads to the production of even less lubrication since the cartilage is in the process of being worn away by the bone movement and deteriorates—a vicious circle.

Arthrosis in its early stages—when damage to the cartilage is slight—is easy to miss until a dog starts showing the first symptoms, usually when the weather is cold and damp. Then, especially first thing in the morning, the dog will show signs of stiffness and will have to warm up first before being able to move easily. If the damage to the cartilage is more advanced, and the thickening of the bone around the affected joint can be seen on an X-ray, then the dog will be in constant pain, even when it is lying down. It will not want to move about much, will avoid certain kinds of movements, or will exhibit signs of lameness.

To diagnose arthrosis, the veterinarian will test the flexibility of the dog's joints and take an X-ray. The goal of any treatment is to stop the degenerative process if possible, or, at the least, to slow it down, and to preserve the dog's mobility and prevent pain. Anti-inflammatory medicines and analgesics are the drugs of choice. In addition, it can be helpful to feed the dog nutritional supplements (see p114). Adequate exercise is also a must in order to strengthen the dog's musculoskeletal system and help keep it in good shape. Physical therapy can also help reduce the symptoms of arthrosis.

Making a diagnosis
The veterinarian thoroughly examines the dog's joints and takes X-rays in order to determine whether or not the senior dog is suffering from arthrosis.

The Spine—Spondylosis Deformans

Degenerative change to the spinal column caused by calcium build-up is known as spondylosis deformans (spondylosis or spinal osteoarthritis). It starts when excess bone grows on the spine (bone spurs), most often toward the front of the dog's body. When this new bone accumulation starts growing on both sides of the spinal column over the disks, two neighboring vertebral segments can become linked together. After this bone overgrowth has calcified completely, and a bridge of bone links the two bones, the dog's pain abates and the affected part of its spine stiffens. Very often, parts of the thoracic or lumbar vertebrae are affected.

Every elderly dog can be affected by spondylosis but some breeds have a greater tendency to this disease. Signs of spondylosis are when the dog's hind legs become lame, it arches its back—almost like a cat, has difficulties getting into a car or going up and down stairs or suddenly cries out when it moves in a certain way. In addition, muscle mass in the thighs of its hind legs shrivels, its gait seems hesitant, its hind legs collapse suddenly, or it drags one of its hind legs. It has difficulty getting up, lying down, or jumping up. When it lies down, it takes a long time to settle into a comfortable position, and it is painful to the dog when you touch it on its back.

There is no known cure for this degenerative disease. The only thing you can do to help your dog is to slow down the progress of the disease. As is the case with arthrosis, anti-inflammatories and analgesics are used to treat a dog suffering from spondylosis. Regular exercise and physical therapy are also crucial in order to preserve the dog's muscles and strengthen them. Homeopathic medicines can also help.

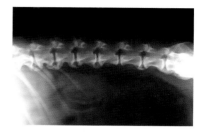

Calcium deposits on the spine
Spondylosis deformans shows up on an X-ray as a bony bridge between two vertebral segments. It is triggered by calcium buildup.

Water gymnastics
in a therapeutic bath gently help make stiff joints fit for action again.

WHAT TO WATCH FOR

There are many different kinds of diseases that can affect a dog's joints and spine and other parts of its musculoskeletal system. Symptoms can include:

→ Lameness (limping, hobbling)

→ Favoring one of its joints

→ Walking stiffly

→ Paws collapse, are dragged along the floor, or drag behind

→ A sudden lack of desire to run and play

→ Sudden whimpers or barks, during play, for example

→ Obvious difficulties getting up, lying down, and climbing stairs

→ Exhibits pain when it is touched in certain ways

→ Problems in defecating or urinating

WATCH OUT FOR THESE SIGNS OF SKIN CHANGES

→ Coat changes color

→ The dog smells more strongly

→ Fatty, oily coat

→ Bald spots

→ Dry or flaky skin

→ Increased sebaceous gland production, infected sebaceous glands

→ Increased wart growth

→ Lipomas (tumors of fat cells)

→ Wounds heal more slowly

WATCH OUT FOR THESE SIGNS OF SKIN CHANGES

→ Coat changes color

→ The dog smells more strongly

→ Fatty, oily coat

→ Bald spots

→ Dry or flaky skin

→ Increased sebaceous gland production, infected sebaceous glands

→ Increased wart growth

→ Lipomas (tumors of fat cells)

→ Wounds heal more slowly

SIGNS OF HEART DISEASE

→ Weakness, fatigue

→ Gets tired easily, can no longer do as much as before

→ Coughing or gagging— especially after exertion and at night

→ Gums turn a bluish color after exertion

→ Has trouble breathing

→ Restlessness at night (lying down compresses the chest)

SKIN AND COAT

When you are petting or brushing or combing your senior dog, always take time to examine its skin (see pp108–114). Pay special attention to areas where there are skin changes you know about already, such as warts or lipomas. If these suddenly begin to grow, harden, bleed, or your dog is scratching them because they are itchy, let your veterinarian know. Some skin problems can be cleared up using medicinal shampoo.

Some skin changes can be a sign of internal disease. For example, bald spots on your dog's coat, extremely thin hair or dandruff can indicate a malfunctioning thyroid gland (see p142). However, if your senior dog develops heavy dandruff within a few seconds after experiencing great excitement do not worry, this is usually normal.

Healthy Grooming
The skin is the body's largest organ. Changes can indicate that your dog is suffering from an illness.

Loss of hair and irritated skin

THE CARDIOVASCULAR SYSTEM

In addition to suffering from genetically determined heart disease, elderly dogs very often experience heart valve problems. The seriousness of the disease varies, and many dogs can live to a ripe old age with proper care.

Heart valve problems

This is most often an acquired vascular disease. It is caused when the edges of the heart valves thicken due to inflammation. As a result, the heart valves no longer meet exactly to form a tight seal and blood flows back into the dog's heart. With the aid of a stethoscope, a veterinarian can clearly hear this backflow of blood as a heart murmur.

When a dog suffers from heart valve disease, its heart starts working less efficiently. It tries to compensate by beating more quickly and strongly (higher pulse rate). The dog's heart has less time to rest between beats, rest the heart needs to ensure its own blood supply. As a result of this irreversible deterioration, blood can start pooling in the heart, eventually ending up in the lungs. Fluid can also build up in the dog's chest or even its abdomen.

If the heart cannot compensate for the damage, it can no longer function properly. The veterinarian diagnoses heart valve disease by listening to the dog's heart, taking X-rays, carrying out an ECG and/or an ultrasound.

Heart diseases such as this are incurable. However, there are drugs available that regulate the heart and increase the amount of stress it can handle. They function by reducing fluid retention, strengthening the heart's contractions, and lowering the pulse rate. The treatment goal is to maintain the current condition as long as possible. With good medical treatment and the right kind of care, a dog suffering from heart disease can live to a ripe old age.

THE ENDOCRINE SYSTEM

Various illnesses that occur in old age are caused by hormonal changes. However, with the right diet and proper medication, most dogs are able to cope well with these illnesses.

Diabetes mellitus

This is a disease that causes glucose (sugar) to build up in a dog's blood due to insufficient insulin production. Insulin is a hormone made in the pancreas. This hormone circulates through a dog's bloodstream along with glucose it ingests in its food, and enables its cells to absorb the glucose's energy. When the pancreas produces insufficient insulin, glucose cannot be absorbed properly by the body's cells and can no longer be used as a source of energy. The excess glucose remains in the dog's blood and its blood sugar level soars as a result. Diabetes mellitus is also known as sugar diabetes. A dog can contract diabetes for a variety of reasons. It might be genetically predisposed to diabetes and its immune system attacks the insulin-producing cells in its pancreas; it might not get enough exercise, be obese, have had certain kinds of infections or have pancreatic tumors.

INSIDE THE HEART

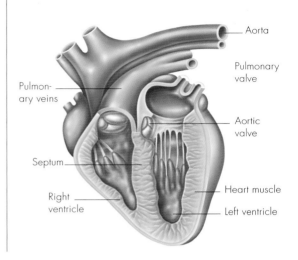

Aorta

Pulmonary valve

Pulmon- ary veins

Aortic valve

Septum

Heart muscle

Right ventricle

Left ventricle

A DOG TALE

When our Afghan Hound Nicky joined our household he was seven years old and we worried because he coughed a lot. The veterinarian discovered that his heart wasn't working effectively. Thanks to a good drug regime and regular checkups, Nicky lived to be thirteen and frolicked about with his friends right up to the end. When he got tired, he took a break. Nicky profited greatly from treatment, and his diseased heart was not the cause of his death.

SIGNS OF DIABETES

→ Increased thirst, excessive urination

→ Nausea, vomiting, and weight loss

→ Fatigue, listlessness, apathy, general weakness

INSULIN CYCLE

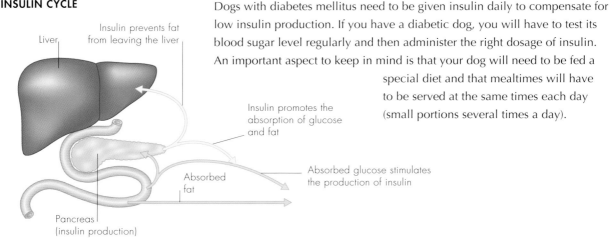

Liver

Insulin prevents fat from leaving the liver

Insulin promotes the absorption of glucose and fat

Absorbed glucose stimulates the production of insulin

Absorbed fat

Pancreas (insulin production)

Dogs with diabetes mellitus need to be given insulin daily to compensate for low insulin production. If you have a diabetic dog, you will have to test its blood sugar level regularly and then administer the right dosage of insulin. An important aspect to keep in mind is that your dog will need to be fed a special diet and that mealtimes will have to be served at the same times each day (small portions several times a day).

The thyroid gland

Usually thyroid problems are caused by hypothyroidism, which means the body does not produce enough thyroid hormones to function properly. Most of the time hypothyroidism is caused when the dog's immune system attacks thyroid cells and destroys them. Some dog breeds have a genetic tendency to this disease. Signs that a dog might have hypothyroidism are if it gains weight, is less energetic than usual, and is listless. Often it will have skin problems as well such as hair loss, colored skin spots on its skin, and skin infections. Sometimes changes in behavior occur such as aggressiveness, fearfulness or excitability, and irritability. Diarrhea is common, too.

To make a diagnosis, the dog's blood tested to determine how much thyroid hormone is being produced. However, tests should also be made of hormones that stimulate the thyroid gland to produce the thyroid hormone. The dog is treated by giving it the correct dosage of the missing hormone.

THE NERVOUS SYSTEM

Degenerative processes can also affect the nervous system and lead to a variety of illnesses.

Canine Cognitive Dysfunction Syndrome (CDS)

The behavior of many elderly dogs changes as they grow old. Some become extremely stubborn; some need a great deal of rest. Others demonstrate even more pronounced behavioral changes and might be suffering from canine cognitive dysfunction syndrome (CDS). When a senior dog has this disease, it loses its cognitive abilities and is no longer able to absorb, process, or

---

SIGNS OF CANINE COGNITIVE DYSFUNCTION (CDS)

→ Loss of orientation, aimlessness

→ Day/night rhythm disturbed (night wandering)

→ Loss of cleanliness (dog gives no signals that it needs "to go", it cannot control urination or defecation)

→ The dog no longer greets people it knows, people are no longer recognized

→ No desire or interest in close contact or being petted

→ Even known situations are "like new'"

→ Intensive, long-lasting whimpering, barking, howling, or shaking without any known reasons

→ Staring into space or corners

Note
Some of these symptoms can also indicate other illnesses.

store new information. This illness is equivalent to Alzheimer's disease in humans. CDS is caused by physiological changes in the dog's brain. Brain cell tissues are damaged and cannot repair themselves, leading to a gradual decline in cognitive abilities. However, it is not always easy to tell if a dog has CDS or is just suffering from age-related dementia or other problems.

In order to make a correct diagnosis, your veterinarian will first have to rule out other illnesses. CDS is treated with special drugs and a special diet. As discussed earlier in this book, all dogs benefit greatly from lifelong mental stimulation (*see p82–85*).

METABOLIC ILLNESSES

As a dog ages, its metabolism slows down—it is no longer as efficient as it once was. This affects some of its organs and the functions they perform.

The liver

The liver is a giant chemical factory, converting substances produced and ingested by the body into different forms the body needs. It is the body's most important detoxifying organ. Acute liver disease, in which the liver is inflamed, is known as hepatitis. It can be caused by infections, or poisoning by drugs or plants, for example. However, wear and tear can also cause liver disease. When a dog contracts acute liver disease, liver cells start to die. Fortunately, the liver is able to regenerate itself. To diagnose liver disease, first the dog's blood is tested; then an X-ray might be taken, an ultrasound is made, or a biopsy (tissue sample) is taken. Treatment consists of drugs and a special diet. In addition, the dog might be given homeopathic or plant-based (phytotherapeutic) medicines.

A long barking session for no clear reason can occur when a dog is suffering from an age-related cognitive disease.

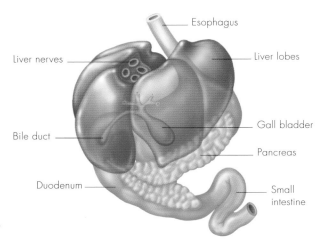

Esophagus

Liver nerves

Liver lobes

Gall bladder

Bile duct

Pancreas

Duodenum

Small intestine

LIVER AND GALL BLADDER

SIGNS OF LIVER DISEASE

→ Vomiting, diarrhea

→ Distaste for food

→ Lack of appetite

→ Yellowish mucous membranes and, perhaps, urine

→ Weakness, apathy

→ Fever

→ Shock (circulatory collapse)

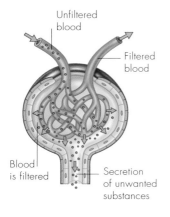

Unfiltered blood

Filtered blood

Blood is filtered

Secretion of unwanted substances

UROGENITAL SYSTEM

Illnesses of the urogenital system usually are specific to a dog's sex.

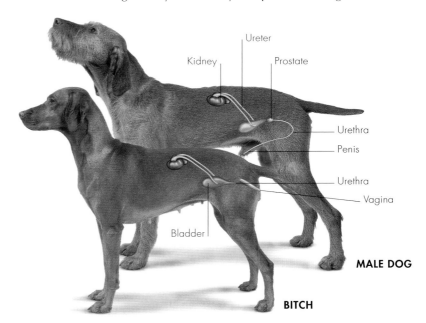

Ureter

Kidney

Prostate

Urethra

Penis

Urethra

Vagina

Bladder

MALE DOG

BITCH

Incontinence

Incontinence refers to involuntary urination, and this most often is seen in neutered dogs or elderly bitches. It is caused by a low estrogen level. In healthy dogs, urine produced by the kidneys is stored in the bladder until the dog voluntarily releases it via the urethra. Usually the sphincter muscle between the bladder and the urethra stays tightly shut, preventing urine from dribbling or flowing out. However, when a dog has a low estrogen level, its sphincter muscle does not stay tightly closed—the dog becomes incontinent. Many bitches are extremely bothered by this situation and find it very unpleasant. This can lead to behavioral changes. And, since urine remains in the urethra, incontinence increases the risk of infection.

Sphincter muscle control is improved by giving the dog estrogen supplements. By no means should you decrease the amount of water you give your bitch to drink! Feed the dog only a moderate amount of food: obesity increases a dog's chances of becoming incontinent.

Medicines used to treat heart disease, such as water pills (diuretics), can increase urine production—then the urge is overwhelming.

Womb Infection (Pyometra)

A womb infection is a life-threatening illness in female dogs. It is caused when bacteria multiply in the dog's womb and secrete pus. There are two types of pyometra. When the dog's cervix remains open—the pus can flow out of the womb through the vagina and out the vulva—it is called open pyometra. When the cervix is tight—the pus cannot flow freely out of the womb—it is called closed pyometra. This bacterial infection can be diagnosed with a blood test and a vaginal swab. Sometimes the veterinarian will also take an X-ray or do an ultrasound examination. Antibiotics can cure this disease in its open form. However, a bitch's womb has to be removed right away if she is suffering from closed pyometra.

THE STOMACH AND INTESTINES

As dogs become elderly, they tend to suffer more from stomach problems and intestinal disorders. Common are constipation, diarrhea, or vomiting (*see p104*). Usually these problems arise because aged dogs tend to get less exercise. In general, lack of activity slows down a dog's digestive processes and reduces its muscle tone. It is important to keep your dog as active as possible and to feed it a fiber-rich diet suited to its age (*see pp99–107*).

Bloat (Gastric Torsion)

Bloat is a life-threatening condition in which gases and fluids build up in a dog's stomach, causing it to swell up. As it swells, the dog's stomach can twist around its long axis. Many things can cause this condition, such as genetic predisposition or age-related loss of elasticity to the tendons that hold up the stomach. Tempestuous activity, such as jumping, boisterous play, or rolling around on a full stomach (also on a water-filled stomach), can lead to gastric torsion—even later on when the dog is resting. Almost in the blink of an eye, the esophagus to the stomach, and the duodenum leading from it, become blocked. The veins that supply blood to the stomach also are blocked and toxic wastes build up rapidly. The dog quickly goes into shock (*see p135*). Its life is at risk and emergency surgery is needed without delay.

SIGNS OF OPEN AND CLOSED PYOMETRA

→ Excessive thirst accompanied by frequent urination

→ Lack of appetite

→ The dog sleeps constantly

→ Fever

→ Vomiting

→ Signs of shock present, blood pressure plummets (*see p135*)

→ A larger increase in size than is normal in pregnancy (in closed pyometra)!

→ Hind legs are weak

SIGNS OF BLOAT / GASTRIC TORSION

→ The stomach swells

→ The dog attempts to vomit unsuccessfully

→ Drooling, retching, groaning

→ Restlessness

Rest after eating
Make sure that your senior dog does not run around or play for two hours after it has eaten.

SIGNS OF TUMORS

→ Increase in size (bumps, pimples, swellings, lumps)

→ Wounds that do not heal properly or do not heal at all

→ Warts or sebaceous glands that change suddenly, grow, or harden

→ Change to the dog's appetite (eats a great deal more or very little), weight change

→ A change in the dog's general health and well-being

Change in size

Constant panting
and half-closed eyes can be an indication that a dog is suffering from pain.

CANCER—TUMORS

Every organ and every system in a dog's body can be affected by cancer. For example, skin, testes, or prostate in a male dog, the milkline (mammary gland tumors) in bitches, and also in male dogs, as well as liver, kidney, spleen, bladder, colon, and the lymphatic system. Depending on the breed, other kinds of tumors can arise.

Cancer is the most common cause of death in dogs. It is caused when tiny cell changes result in the malignant, uncontrolled, growth of tumors. Some tumors are benign such as those that can grow on the anal sac glands of male dogs that have not been castrated (see p121).

Depending on the type of tumor, and its size, there are different kinds of treatments available such as chemotherapy or surgical removal. If your dog is very old, you and your veterinarian should discuss frankly whether it is better to treat the tumor or to make the dog's remaining time as comfortable as possible, by pain management, for example.

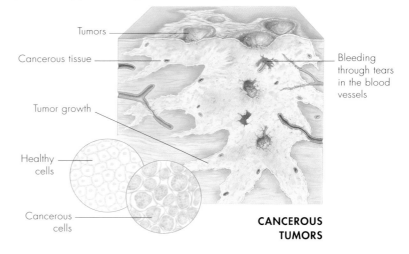

Tumors

Cancerous tissue

Bleeding through tears in the blood vessels

Tumor growth

Healthy cells

Cancerous cells

CANCEROUS TUMORS

PAIN TREATMENT—PAIN MANAGEMENT

Pain signals the body that it needs to protect itself or serves as a warning. A dog's quality of life is greatly reduced by the chronic pain accompanying illnesses such as joint or spinal disease. We believe that when an aged dog is suffering from pain, we should free it as best we can from this pain. Today, medications exist that can alleviate chronic pain throughout the day. A dog owner must weigh the risks involved in giving a senior dog pain relief with the help of the veterinarian. The goal of pain management should be to give the dog a pleasant life to the end while taking its needs into account.

Some drugs have known side effects. However, these would only begin to have a negative effect on the dog after the projected life span of the dog had been reached. The dog would be dead before any side effects set in. If this is the case, treating a dog with these drugs is an acceptable risk.

THE SENSES

A dog's powers of sight and hearing can deteriorate significantly as it grows older. Often a dog owner does not notice the early signs that its senses are failing, or explains them away as something else, such as stubbornness, when the dog no longer responds reliably to commands (see p94). If this describes your canine friend, then take it to the veterinarian so a proper diagnosis can be made.

Deteriorating vision

When a dog no longer sees well, it will often seem uncertain or hesitant when walking or climbing stairs. Usually you first will notice this at twilight. Some dogs trip frequently, others bump against objects, such as furniture.

Lens sclerosis: As a dog ages, its eye lenses become less flexible. They harden and take on a bluish grayish color. This is a natural part of the aging process and is usually seen in dogs who are nine years or older although it can set in earlier or later than this. Some dogs develop farsightedness as a result of this condition.

Cataract: A cataract causes the proteins in an eye's lens to harden. The lens becomes cloudy and loses its transparency. The cloudiness can affect a lens in part or in whole. A dog is genetically predisposed to cataracts, although they can also be caused by metabolic diseases, such as diabetes. This disease starts slowly in the affected eye with a gradual loss of sight that leads to blindness. Cataracts are diagnosed by a simple eye examination. Surgery restores, or improves, a dog's sight.

Impaired hearing

Impaired hearing, which can progress to deafness when a dog is aged, is a normal part of the aging process. Dogs with impaired hearing can become hesitant, and they often react too late to danger. Try a little hearing test: does your dog still react when you shake the treat bag?

HOW DO I RECOGNIZE PAIN IN A DOG?

To do this, you will have to interpret your dog's behavior. Signs your dog is in pain are, among others, rapid breathing, whimpering and sighing, howling, groaning, crying out, shivering, dilated pupils, chattering teeth, restlessness, pacing, and sudden aggressive behavior. Some dogs that are in pain cannot lie down or sit still in one position for very long and so appear to be restless. If you observe any of these signs in your dog, bring it to the veterinarian as quickly as you can.

Cataract
A lens clouds up due to protein deposits in the lens. The only treatment for a cataract is an eye operation.

Despite impaired vision, senior dogs can derive much pleasure from life and still experience exciting adventures.

Injected anesthetics

ANESTHETICS

The reason a dog is given anesthetics is to shut down all its senses and reactions and to eliminate pain. When it has been anesthetized, a dog is sedated. It is unconscious and feels no pain, and its muscles are relaxed.

Anesthetics used in veterinary medicine are being constantly improved so that even older dogs, or those already suffering from an illness (risk patients) can be gently sedated. Which method will be used on your dog is decided on according to the length of the operation, the procedure used, the size of the area being operated on and the overall condition of the patient.

The dog sleeps
and feels no pain. Ointment protects the dog's eyes from drying out during the operation.

TYPES OF ANESTHETIC	
There are various methods of administering anesthetics. They include:	
Injection	The anesthetic drugs are injected under the skin, into a muscle, or into a vein.
Inhalation	First the dog is injected with a preanesthetic so that an endotracheal tube can be introduced into its windpipe. During the operation, the tube is used to administer anesthetics using steam or gas and to give the dog oxygen. With this method, the dog can be dosed precisely and it is easy on patients suffering from a preexisting disease such as heart disease.
Local anesthesia	Local anesthesia deadens reaction to pain. This type of anesthetic is used for minor operations such as the removal of skin tumors. The canine patient is conscious the entire time. In human medicine, local anesthetics are used for dental procedures or when wounds are stitched up, for example.

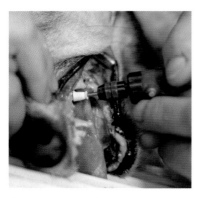

The veterinarian begins to work
and the dog is unaware of anything. If the procedure takes longer, more anesthetics can be administered.

PREPARATION FOR ANESTHETICS

A thorough examination beforehand and proper preparation minimize the risks that are associated with anesthetics. Various factors such as the dog's age, previous illnesses, allergies, overall condition, and its past reaction to anesthetics are taken into account. Senior dogs, especially, should be given a checkup ahead of time, and up-to-date blood-tests (including liver and kidney analysis) are highly recommended.

Do not feed your dog for twelve hours before an operation—not even a dog biscuit or a tiny treat—in order to prevent it from choking on its own vomit during surgery. Since the organs of elderly dogs cannot break down anesthetics very quickly because they work less efficiently than those of younger dogs, giving them a lower dosage of the anesthetic and an intravenous drip during surgery will reduce the risks.

POSTANESTHETIC CARE

After you bring home a dog that has been given anesthetics during surgery, allow it to sleep off the effects of the drugs in peace and quiet. Make sure not to put it on a raised surface so that it cannot fall down. If it is used to a carrier, putting the dog in a dog carrier to sleep off the drugs is ideal. Since anesthetics cause the body's temperature to sink, choose a warm, cozy, and quiet spot for your dog and cover it with a blanket. When the canine patient has awakened fully, allow it to eat a small amount of food that same evening; if in doubt, wait until the next morning. Your dog is permitted a drink as soon as it is able to walk over to its water bowl. Many dogs start licking at their wound or biting it right away. Some are extremely tenacious, even when the wound is well bandaged and a protective jacket or T-shirt covers it; they endanger themselves. These dogs will need to wear a plastic funnel or Elizabethan collar, which you can get from the veterinarian, or make yourself, so that the wound can heal and infections can be avoided. Usually a dog readily adapts to an Elizabethan collar in a very short time.

After an operation
an Elizabethan collar prevents a dog from licking the wound and dissolving the stitches holding it together.

DOGS AT RISK

→ Short-nosed dogs

→ Obese dogs

→ Dogs with liver/kidney disease

→ Dogs with heart disease

→ Diabetic and epileptic dogs

→ Previous problems with anesthetics

Loving care
After anesthesia a dog should be allowed to sleep peacefully. Keep noise and stress away from it.

"I have sometimes thought of the final cause of dogs having such short lives and I am quite satisfied it is in compassion to the human race; for if we suffer so much in losing a dog after an acquaintance of ten or twelve years, what would it be were they to live double that time?"

Walter Scott (1771–1832)

SAD FAREWELLS

FROM THE VERY FIRST DAY a puppy or an elderly dog is bought into its new home, a dog owner is aware that, at some point, the time will come to say farewell. Everyone hopes that this final phase will be a relatively painless one for both dog and human.

Unfortunately, this is not always destined to be, especially when the death of a dog is preceded by a long and difficult illness. As a dog owner lovingly cares for his or her dog during its final illness, both family members and other dog lovers must rally to provide support at this time, especially if you have decided to euthanize your dog.

It is terribly difficult to part with an old canine friend, but the wonderful times you have spent together should not be overshadowed by this last phase of its life. Remember the joyful times you have spent together. Life with a dog is bounded by time, but love for a dog has no limits.

WHEN THE END IS NEAR

Every dog
should be allowed to age with dignity. When its time has come, allow your dog go to its final resting place.

Very few dogs remain fit and healthy into old age; many grow ill or become very fragile. A dog owner has a responsibility to make the animal as comfortable as possible, enabling it to live a full life to the end.

WHEN IS LIFE WORTH LIVING?

If a dog is not released naturally from pain and suffering, its human will have to make the difficult decision when and how to end its life.

The dog's well-being

As their canine friends age, it is likely that all dog owners will have to ask themselves if there is any quality to their dogs' lives. There are many different criteria people apply to determine this. For some, a dog is still enjoying life if, with great effort and although it can hardly get up on its legs, it wags its tail when spoken to by its owner. Others say their dog has no quality-of-life when it no longer can take part in the family's daily life, is incontinent, or cannot get up without assistance. These examples show that there are no hard and fast rules about what constitutes quality of life. Any final decision can only be made on the basis of personal experience and feelings.

Your family's well-being

Caring for a severely ill dog can be an enormous burden on the whole family. Has the dog needed round-the-clock care over a period of several weeks, or even months? Is there any chance of improvement? Ask yourself if it might not be in the best interest of both animal and human to have the veterinarian bring the situation to a close.

Try to remain objective

In order to help yourself decide what kind of quality-of-life your dog has, ask yourself the following questions:

- Is the dog suffering from pain that cannot be alleviated?
- If regular treatment is necessary, is it very stressful or painful for the dog?
- Can you and your family no longer afford to continue paying for the dog's medical treatments?

LETTING YOUR DOG "GO"

If you have answered "yes" to one of these questions, then sadly the time has come to start thinking about euthanasia. This is by far the most difficult moment in a dog-owner's life and, from our own experience, we strongly recommend seeking out the advice and support of a veterinarian at this time. No one other than the dog's owner can make the final decision. However, someone who is at a distance from the situation but who feels the same way about dogs as you do, and is knowledgeable about them, can provide valuable input and help in the decision-making process.

Different points of view

It is hard enough to reach a decision on one's own; often it is even more difficult for a family to reach a consensus. Frequently, opinions vary widely, especially between those family members who spend a great deal of time with the dog, and those who are away from home all day. In our opinion, the person who is closest to the dog and cares for it the most should be the one whose opinion carries the most weight.

Dignity and respect

During any deliberations about putting a dog to sleep, two things always should be kept paramount: making sure the dog does not suffer, and allowing it to keep its dignity. This means showing the dog respect. It also means that personal needs must be set aside and the dog is not held on to for too long. Misguided animal love and egotism are not needed here.

It is often very difficult
to decide whether a dog has quality-of-life or should be put to sleep by the veterinarian.

CHILDREN

Whether or not you involve your child in the decision to euthanize the family dog depends on the child's age, maturity, and relationship to the dog. Unfortunately, there is no ready-made formula. Each child reacts to and processes the situation differently. When parents provide honest and clear explanations, many children handle the decision-making process amazingly well. For others, it is kinder not to tell them that the dog has been euthanized, and to leave them in the belief that their good old friend died in its sleep quietly and peacefully, and without human assistance.

Parents often find
it difficult to tell their children about the approaching death of a beloved family dog.

THE LAST LOVING ACT

Before you make the final decision to euthanize a much-loved dog, you and your family will experience many emotional ups and downs.

Despite this emotional roller-coaster ride, you must try to keep a cool head since every hour a dog has to suffer without hope of relief is torture to it! Once the decision to euthanize your dog has been reached, you should quickly discuss with your veterinarian how it will be put to sleep. Many veterinarians will come to the home to put a dog to sleep. As a dog lies in its dog bed, it is gently put to sleep.

FAREWELL TO A FRIEND

It is important that every dog owner finds a personal way of saying goodbye to his or her steadfast companion. Many are comforted by enjoying a last walk with their dog, spending an hour cuddling with it or just by simply spending an evening with their dog on the sofa. You will not be able to hide your mood from your dog entirely. Its senses and ability to register emotions are much more developed than those of human beings. However, at this significant time—just as when the dog is euthanized—a dog's human should be demonstrating strength. So that the dog does not begin to sense that something bad is going to happen soon, you must not behave hesitantly or sadly around it. It is better to use the remaining time to revue the happy times you and your dog have spent together.

All dog owners should see it as a matter of honor to ensure that the dog's most-trusted human, or even the whole family, is present at the death of their loyal companion. We must not leave a beloved dog alone in its final hours—perhaps even in a strange setting!

Every dog owner knows that at some point it will be time to say goodbye. But when the moment has come, no one is properly prepared.

TYPES OF BURIAL

Burying a loyal canine friend is part of the mourning process for many. For some, the dog lives on in primarily in their memories; others need a specific physical place, such as a grave, in order to feel close to their dog. More and more dog owners are choosing to give their dogs a dignified burial. The respect and affection a dog owner had for a dog when it was alive should be reflected in the way it is buried.

EUTHANASIA— THE "GOOD DEATH"

In the original Greek, euthanasia means "good death" (*eu*: beautiful, good, *thanatos*: death). Every dog owner should allow a suffering dog a gentle death. In fact, animal protection laws prohibit anyone from causing an animal to suffer unnecessarily. When a dog is euthanized, an overdose of anesthetic is injected into its veins. The dog quickly loses consciousness and dies. Sometimes a sedative is administered in advance.

Removal by the veterinarian

If it is your wish, your veterinarian will arrange to have your dog's body cremated and its ashes returned to you, or will arrange for its body to be disposed of by an animal disposal company.

Home burial

For public health reasons, not every jurisdiction permits you to bury dogs or other animals on your property. Your veterinarian will most likely know what the regulations are in your area, or you can check with the local authorities. If you would like an exception to be made ask the local authorities if this is possible and get written permission where required.

Pet cemetery

Not every dog owner has a garden but many have a strong need to bury their dog's body or its ashes (*see below*). Pet cemeteries, which sell burial plots and arrange funerals, address this need. The cost of burying a pet varies from cemetery to cemetery and, as with human burial, is determined by several factors. These include the type of grave (mass or individual), the kind of casket (or urn) you choose, the size of the plot, the elaborateness of the grave marker, the type of funeral you want, and whether or not you opt for grave maintenance—and for how long. It is best to call several pet cemeteries located in your area in order to compare costs and to find out which resting-place best suits your requirements. Do not hesitate to ask if you have a special wish!

Cremation

Pet cremation is a popular method of dealing with a pet's remains. Here, you can choose between mass and individual cremation. If you decide on the latter, your dog's ashes will be placed in a small cardboard box, or urn, and given to you. You can then decide what you would like to do with the ashes. Some opt to store the ashes at home in a decorative urn. Others scatter the ashes in their garden, or in a pet cemetery scatter garden. Scattering animal ashes in nature is not allowed in every jurisdiction so check with your local authorities or veterinarian to find out about the regulations in your area. In a pet cemetery, you can also purchase a niche in which to place your dog's ashes, or have the ashes placed in a common grave. The pet cemetery will provide you with a wide variety of burial options ranging from the type of funeral service to the size of the niche and type of niche marker.

ANIMAL FUNERAL SERVICES

Many companies will arrange your pet's burial down to the last detail—from picking up its body to burying it with all due ceremony. Not only does it pay to compare prices, but to ask about possible extra costs. For example, are grave maintenance fees included in the plot price or are they extra? You can get information from the local animal protection association, your veterinarian, and the Internet.

Today, many beautiful pet cemeteries allow you to bury your beloved dog with due ceremony.

An urn with the ashes of your dog can only be given to you if your dog has been individually cremated.

A TIME FOR MOURNING

Being comforted by good friends helps alleviate the sorrow after the loss of a dog. Children, in particular, need a great deal of attention at this time.

The death of a dog that shared both times of joy and suffering over the years is a very difficult thing for most people to come to terms with.

Especially those people whose dog was their main companion and social contact suffer enormously. The way each person deals with the death of a beloved dog is very different. It is important, no matter what the circumstances, to be able to give one's grief free reign.

BEING COMFORTED

After their dog has died a natural death or been euthanized, many people torture themselves with feelings of guilt. They blame themselves, or other family members, for not seeing a disease in time, or not recognizing that mistakes have been made in treating the dog for an illness. In order that these guilt feelings do not become all-consuming, it is important to talk to other dog owners and feeling friends about your experiences. Never forget that mourning is a natural thing to do. One should never be ashamed of mourning for a dog or let oneself be irritated by remarks made by ignorant or insensitive people such as "After all, it was only a dog!" Time to mourn is important. After all, the deceased was not "just" a dog, but also a good friend.

COMFORTING CHILDREN

In order to say goodbye properly, children often find it very helpful to take part in a funeral service for a dead pet. Small children might need the help of a mental picture in order to visualize what death is. Perhaps they can be comforted by the thought that a "dog heaven" exists, or by some other kind of religious thought, depending on their faith. Talking about a dog that has died should never be forbidden; sharing memories of the dog with each another is an important part of coping. To a child, losing a childhood dog is a very significant milestone in its life and it will always remember the feelings it had during this important event.

HOW OTHER DOGS REACT

The way another dog that shares your home reacts to the death of one of its own kind varies greatly from dog to dog. Often, it depends on the kind of relationship the dogs had with one another.

If the deceased dog was an important authority figure for the remaining dog, giving it strength and keeping it well grounded, it will dearly miss its canine companion. Some dogs will creep off to be alone, have very little appetite and be hard to engage in any kind of activity; some even are thrown completely off-kilter. If this is the case, you will have to keep the dog busy, provide it with a sense of security (*see p86*) and help it find its own path given the changed circumstances.

If the two dogs merely tolerated each other's existence, living alongside rather than with one another, it might be that your remaining dog goes about its daily business as though nothing has happened, and shows no reaction whatsoever. This, too, is normal behavior.

There are also dogs that only come into their own after the death of another dog because they were not as free to do what they wanted to do before. Do not be disappointed, this is not a sign of heartlessness. It is simply a sign that the dog has adjusted to the new situation.

Sometimes it is hard
to judge how a dog will behave after its canine companion has died.

AN EMPTY SPOT

"I will never own a dog again—its death was just too hard on me!" is often the first thought that dog owners have after their four-legged friends have died. However, very few bereaved dog owners actually carry through with this resolve. In our experience, the speed with which a new dog is acquired after the death of another varies greatly. Some people cannot stand a quiet house, an empty dog bed, or a radical change to their routine, and begin the quest for a new dog almost immediately. Others need to mourn for months, perhaps even years, before there is room in their hearts for a new dog. There is no right or wrong way to react. It only is important not to treat the new dog as a replacement for the old, but to accept it for itself as a being with its own personality. Continually comparing a new dog to an old one will lead to frustration on all sides—every dog is unique, possessing its own strengths, talents, and endearing qualities that are waiting to be discovered and nourished. You will best honor your previous dog by cherishing its memory and learning from the experiences you had with it. Your new dog will profit enormously.

A small bundle of energy
brings action back into the house! If you and your senior dog had been used to a well-regulated and quiet life, you will have to look sharp! A new puppy demands almost round-the-clock attention from its new human family.

INDEX

ACKNOWLEDGMENTS

It is a long time between the conception and realization of a book and we would like to give heartfelt thanks to all those who have accompanied us on this journey.

Ines Röger-Diehl (Dillenburg, Germany), the dog-trainer Anne Neumann (Vancouver, Canada), Mathias Nagengast (Lichtenfels, Germany), the veterinarians Stefanie Hallack (Weilburg, Germany), Katja Hinderink (Tolkkinen, Finland), Tanja Hiepler (Rees, Germany), Dr. med. vet. Ariane Volpert (Bad Soden, Germany) and Dr. med. vet. Christiane Cleff-Matzak (Dreikirchen, Germany) as well as the animal physiotherapist Eva Müller (Germany) for their professional expertise and their extensive and constructive comments on the text, the Tierarztpraxis Dr. Johann Geuting (Animal Medicine Practice of Dr. Johann Geuting, Isselburg, Germany), the Veterinary Clinic Ketter (Veterinary Clinic, Löhnberg, Germany), the Reha-Zentrum für Kleintiere der Tierklinik Hofheim (Small Animal Rehabilitation Center in the Hofheim Veterinary Clinic, Hofheim, Germany), Trimsalon Imladris (Dog Beauty Salon, Dinxperlo, Netherlands) and the Tierfriedhof Frankfurt am Main (Pet Cemetery, Rödelheim, Germany) for their kind permission to take photographs in their establishments, and our four-legged senior models, their younger friends, and humans for patiently letting themselves be photographed and for having fun doing it. The oldest dog pictured is 18 years old and we were able to show the entire spectrum of elderly dogs. We got to know many wonderful people and dogs and were often very impressed with the great dedication with which people cared for their aged dogs. Some of the dogs in this book have died since it was published; these we would remember here.

Heike Schmidt-Röger would especially like to thank her husband Stefan for his patience, understanding and support, and her mother for the constant encouragement to write and photograph.

Of course we must not forget the four-legged friends that gave us so much inspiration, joy and challenge: the Afghan Hounds Nicky and Shalim, the Dachshunds Gina and Paul, the Ibizan Podenco bitches Lena and Puriah, the Golden Retriever-Mix Joschi, and Kate the Whippet. Some came into our lives when they were already aged, others grew old in our care. We have already had to say farewell to Gina, Nicky and Lena—thank you for the time we spent together.

Finally, our thanks go to the Dorling Kindersley team in Starnberg, in particular the program director Monika Schlitzer, who placed her trust in us, the graphic designer Verena Salm for realizing the layout and our editor Regina Franke, who with great friendliness, professionality, and dog knowledge supported and steered this endeavor.

PICTURE CREDITS
All photograhs not listed below were taken by Heike Schmidt-Röger, Herborn, Germany.

The publisher would like to thank the following people for their kind permission to use their photographs:

t=top, tc=top center, b=below, r=right, l=left, c=center, DT=dog tale, CT=cutout

Susanne Blank, Sulzbach, Germany: p34; p53t, c; p56; p77b; p79t; p82t; p101CT; p113CT; p114CT, b; p135t, b; p130b; p155t. Stefanie Hallack, Weilburg, Germany: p24DT; p36DT; p67; p87DT; p138t; p139t; p147b. Katja Hinderink, Tolkkinen, Finland: p21DT; p57DT; p88. Monika Schlitzer, Munich, Germany: p41.

Dorling Kindersley Image Archive
Photographs: p14b; p30b; p35bl, bc; p37t; p39tc; p40t; p63b; p65b.
Illustrations: p98b; p110b; p121; p133c, CT; p136; p137b.; p140cr; p141t; p142t; p143b; p144t; p146cr; p156b.